THE SEA COMMONWEALTH

A

35361

THE IMPERIAL STUDIES SERIES

THE SEA COMMONWEALTH

AND OTHER PAPERS

EDITED BY

A. P. NEWTON, M.A., D.Lit., B.Sc.

Essay Index Reprint Series

Originally published by:
J. M. DENT & SONS LTD.

BOOKS FOR LIBRARIES PRESS, INC.
FREEPORT, NEW YORK

First Published 1919
Reprinted 1968

Reprinted from a copy in the collections of
The New York Public Library
Astor, Lenox and Tilden Foundations

LIBRARY OF CONGRESS CATALOG CARD NUMBER:

68-22114

PRINTED IN THE UNITED STATES OF AMERICA

PREFATORY NOTE

THE papers that are here collected were originally delivered as lectures in an Imperial Studies course in the University of London, King's College, during the Session 1917-18. The original title of the course was "The Empire and the Outer World," and it was designed to draw the attention of its hearers from an excessive preoccupation with the momentous events taking place on the continent of Europe to a remembrance that Britain's true concern is rather with the affairs of the world as a whole than with the narrower details of purely territorial questions with which the land powers of Europe are so intimately concerned. Unavoidable difficulties prevented the course having so great a unity of subject and treatment as is usually aimed at by the Imperial Studies Committee, but the papers contain so much of interest in themselves that it has been thought well to collect and publish them in a companion volume to others in the Imperial Studies Series.

While the volume was passing through the press the ranks of higher journalism sustained a serious loss through the untimely death of Mr. J. E. Mackenzie, one of the last of whose tasks was the correction of the proofs of his article on "The Colonial Aspirations of Germany." It is impossible to put forth these pages without a word of sincere regret for the passing of so accomplished a collaborator.

A. P. N.

UNIVERSITY OF LONDON,
  KING'S COLLEGE,
    March, 1919.

CONTENTS

THE SEA COMMONWEALTH
AND OTHER PAPERS

CHAPTER I

THE SEA COMMONWEALTH
By SIR JULIAN CORBETT, LL.M., F.S.A.

THE war has fallen like a veil between us and the future. Never, perhaps, has it been more difficult to see beyond the tumult of passing events, and never has it been of more vital consequence to keep sure hold of the well-tried guiding lines, lest when the veil is lifted we fail to distinguish the path of our destiny. Already we are dimly conscious that new cross-tracks have obscured it, that new obstacles have arisen through which we must find a way, and that in the company of our guides there is anxious and uncertain whispering.

Amongst all that is obscure, nothing is more disturbing, nothing more difficult to penetrate than the future of the Empire. What will it be? What changes shall we see arising out of the new forces and resistances which the war has engendered? We feel but cannot measure them; we can only tentatively guess what will be the resultant directions of the new strains. Yet while we are conscious that the Empire can never be the same again, that it will be something more complex, more difficult to control, yet it seems plain that

there are some elements which cannot change if it is to
exist as one healthy organism ; and it is upon these
that we must endeavour to keep our hold.

First among them is this—that whatever else the
Empire may become, it must be a Sea Commonwealth.
It was always so, and the developments which the war
has been forcing towards maturity all tend to emphasise
that conception of the Empire as the fundamental fact.
If we look back a little, we realise that as each member
of the Empire became more and more conscious of its
individual existence, more and more bent on self-
expression in its internal growth, the sea became more
and more the influence which checked and balanced
the centrifugal forces that were set up. To those forces
the war, so far as we can see, will have added new
activity. We must at least face the probability that
those forces will no longer be a question of internal
concern. It may well be that the great members of the
family will appear, when the veil is lifted, as separate
centres of foreign policy. We may have to recognise a
Pacific centre, a South African centre and a Canadian
centre, besides the old Home centre, and India may
well become more markedly than before a centre of its
own. Should anything of this kind be found to have
eventuated when the horizon is clear again—and to
some extent at least it must be so—the centrifugal
tendencies cannot fail to exhibit increased energy. To
those whose eyes have not been blinded by the tremendous flashing of the central theatre to what has
been going on in the outer fringes of the war, the outlook is fraught with danger—a new danger which might
well cause hearts to fail, were it not that the germ of

dissolution carries with it its own antidote. For however particularist, however divergent in tendency may be the reactions from these new centres of foreign policy, they must one and all be dependent in the last resource upon sea power ; and since in this connection at least the sea is all one, the old bond of union reasserts itself more strongly than ever. It is given a new meaning, a new force and a new indispensability which no sagacious particularism can afford to disregard.

Nor is it only from the security which sea power alone can give that the centripetal force will draw its vitality. For sea power to be of sufficient strength to afford a sure basis for the common life, it can only be produced by a united effort of the whole organism. No part or group of parts enjoys resources enough without the rest. Each must accept its function in the common task, each must sacrifice so much of its individuality as is needed for just co-ordination of the work, and in joint labour and sacrifice is ever found the surest bond of union.

So far then—if the essential condition of the Sea Commonwealth be admitted—we can face with confidence the half-seen shapes that loom ominously in the obscurity that shrouds the future. But these aspects of the cloudy problem—the aspects which directly concern our own task and conduct—are but half the tangled factors. Instinctively we feel that in some form or other the continued existence of our vast commonwealth depends on supreme sea power. Reason, as dispassionate as we are able to bring to bear, and the functional effect of centuries of experience, will alike forbid us to think otherwise, and yet if the world of the future is to

be something better than a vast armed camp, how will
the rest of humanity be brought to endure what to us
is the essential postulate of our continued existence as
a family of free nations? We honestly believe that the
British Empire, so conceived, makes for the peace of the
world and the comity of universal intercourse. But that
is a view we cannot hope to see universally accepted.
For the greater part of the world the British Empire is
an overpowering combination which is solely moved
by lust of dominion and greedy self-interest. For us it
is a league of nations preoccupied with reconciling conflicting interests by mutual concession and understanding. But till others can see our Commonwealth as we
see it, our supreme sea power must always be a burden
under which they will chafe. They will endure it only
with a resentment that will continue to endanger peace.

And yet for a century it has been endured—for a
century in constant labour with the birth of new
nations, and the rebirth of others, a century which has
tended to enlarge continually the arena of possible conflict as the higher civilisations quickened the dead and
dark regions of the earth. Through such a burning
century it has been endured, at least with grudging
acquiescence, and if in the face of energetic national
movement and expansion it met with no irreconcilable
opposition, it can only be because it was felt on the
whole to be a convenience to the world. Certainly it
was not employed, as it might have been, to thwart the
spirit of the age. In the first hours of its triumph
Napoleon wondered at the moderation with which it
was used, and could never understand why we did not
seize the moment to close the Eastern seas to all but

ourselves. We were too old and wise not to profit by the example of other fallen empires which, in seeking strength by exclusion, found their death. We used our power instead to smooth the paths of commerce for all men to the furthest corners of the earth, and we used it to foster the growth of the struggling nations that were springing up in the New World as well as the Old. Side by side with the new births, our own Colonies grew into nations and our Empire spread, but everywhere the British flag was planted all men, no matter whence they hailed, were free to come and go, free to trade as they would, free to gather and enjoy what they could find, as though it was their own country that had spread the quickening force. So it was that our sea power was felt as a convenience to the world, and so we must use it if we would have it tolerated in the changing future into which we are striving to see.

It may not be easy. As we seek to guide our ship through the dangers that loom ahead, temptations arise to try methods we have long abandoned. We begin to lose faith in the old seamanship by which we weathered former storms. We incline to distrust the strength of bonds that have hitherto held our craft together. Most insistent of these temptations is the lure of fiscal bonds. It is vaguely felt that by some fiscal union within the Commonwealth its fabric could be made stronger and more compact, and its power of resistance to attack increased. And nowhere is the temptation more strongly felt than amongst those who would also preserve our sea power in its most formidable shape. It may be they are right—it may be that some form of fiscal union will prove inevitable or at least expedient for a time. That is a matter of high controversy with which there is no need to deal in this place. But it is necessary to point out that, right or wrong, it is a pregnant departure from all the old principles by which we made the Empire felt as a convenience to the world. Fiscal union within the Commonwealth, whatever strength it may bring, must mean restriction of trade to those who are not within the family. It would mean that, over the great proportion of the earth which we have absorbed, men would not be free to enjoy the fruits of the soil as they have been hitherto. Our Sea Commonwealth would at once become a burden to the nations, and we could no longer look even for the grudging acquiescence with which our sea power has so long been tolerated.

Let there be then no misunderstanding. However strong the bond of sea power, however strong the bond of fiscal union, the forces on which their strength depends do not pull in the same direction. Their binding and resisting energy is not the sum of their individual energies. The one tends to weaken the other, and it does so because it tends to raise forces of counter-resistance. It is an old maxim of strategy—and one that the present war has proved up to the hilt—that if possible we should never use a plan of campaign which tends to raise up new forces against us. Now whatever new strength we might gain by fiscal union, this is certain, that it would raise up new antagonisms to the measures on which we have hitherto successfully relied. Our sea power would at once become an irritant. Instead of being an influence from which the majority of men could feel they were drawing an advantage, it would be seen as a tyranny—and it is as a tyranny that those who seek to supplant us are trying to make the world see it. So far, at least, we should be playing into their hands, and in the end, however much we might hope by fiscal measures to give a new solidity to our Commonwealth, we should be making not for strength but for weakness.

This aspect of the problem is one that scarcely ever appears in Imperial discussion. Without in any way prejudging the merits of Imperial Preference and kindred expedients for giving a new cohesion and unity to our League of British Nations, and without for a moment forgetting how strong is the case for fostering essential industries, still it must be said that the incalculable reactions of these far-reaching measures on the vital question of British naval predominance are too often forgotten. Possibly it is that we are inclined to take that predominance too easily, as an unalterable phenomenon. Of late years we have come to regard the sea as the matrix in which the mosaic of our Empire is set, and in contemplating the whole resplendent design we are apt to take the bed in which it rests as a matter of course, and to assume that we can modify the design to any extent without fear of disintegrating the matrix. It is a dangerous assumption, more dangerous now than ever, since new Sea Powers have grown up, and new resistances to our naval predominance are arising out of vague aspirations for disarmament and what is called Freedom of the Seas. Hitherto we have gone easily forward on the simple principle that at sea we must be absolutely safe, ignoring the correlative fact that when one Power is absolutely safe there must always be others who will feel themselves unsafe. A tendency is consequently set up for these Powers to coalesce in order to bring about something more like equilibrium. Great power is apt to breed great resistance, and sea power is no exception to the rule. Through the din of the past troubled years we have heard the grinding of those resistances, and be sure we shall hear them with greater insistence when the war is done. We recognise the sound of them not only in the two vague expressions, " Disarmament " and " Freedom of the Seas," but also in the much more practical one, " The Open Door," and this is one which we cannot pass over as an impossible dream.

Till quite recent years we kept the principle of the open door sacred and untouched—that is, ever since we discovered that our old Colonial system was not the unmixed blessing we expected it to be. The doors of our ports, as they sprang into existence all over the world, were as open to our neighbours as to ourselves. They were true open doors through which all men were given new and free access to the long-hidden resources of the earth, and the ways to them were charted and kept open for mankind by our Fleet. The result was that the growth of the Empire was for long so little noticed as a political phenomenon, that the bulk of the work was done before the world realised what it meant as a factor in international life. When their eyes were opened they were surprised, even irritated ; but since all doors stood open the practical result was found to be an increase in the field of free and equal commerce. It was regarded on the whole—grudgingly, it may be— as a convenience, and by the older and saner of our neighbours, at least, it was felt as something to be rivalled but not to need disturbing.

But what will be the feeling when they see the doors even partially closed ?—and closed not merely throughout the old Empire, but over an Empire which, as well may be, will have covered vast new tracts of the earth and immeasurable new fields of those raw materials which every day become more essential to the needs of modern civilised life. It cannot but be that new or more formidable resistances to our Commonwealth and the sea power that is its life will be set up, and it may be that in setting them up we shall have released forces more powerful than any that it is in our power to develop for withstanding them. Then too late we shall look back with regret to the sober wisdom of our fathers, who knew their strength and its limitations, and, rich in that wisdom, established the Empire as all their sons have quietly enjoyed it.

In approaching the unsolved problems that lie indistinctly before us, let us then never for a moment forget what is the main force on which our Commonwealth rests, and upon which, so far as human eyes can see, it must always rest. Let us beware of committing ourselves to work which may sap the foundations so surely laid by centuries of sagacious restraint. If we would live, we must let live. If we would see our Commonwealth quietly accepted in the international system, let us do our best to persuade men that it is to their advantage as well as our own that it should exist. If it is to exist, it can only be as a Sea Commonwealth, and sea power will be its life-blood. To that condition the nations must be reconciled. Can we hope that they will be reconciled, if so vast a measure of sea power is tainted with restriction of trade ?

Amongst the members of our Commonwealth it is mutual concession, mutual sympathy and mutual assistance that have cemented the loose-jointed fabric that our ancestors built up. Let us read the lesson into our relations with the outside world, and keep them firmly in mind as we seek to fix our place amongst the nations when the chaos of the war takes shape again.

CHAPTER II

FRANCE AND COLONIAL POWER

By PROF. PAUL MANTOUX, D-ès-L.

Professor of French History and Institutions in the University
of London

A SHORT time before the Franco-German War of 1870,
Prévost Paradol, one of the most promising men of the
younger generation, was surveying with a far-seeing
eye the situation in Europe and the future of his own
country. He could see the war coming, " France and
Prussia running against each other like two express
trains which cannot be stopped." He was afraid of
possible consequences, and also of the grave problem
opened by the declining birth-rate of the French population. But he pointed to one bright spot : in North
Africa, France had laid for herself the foundations of a
great and prosperous Empire. There a new France,
La France Nouvelle—such was the title of his book
—was to find fresh sources of wealth, energy and
greatness.

The suggestion has been followed up by the statesmen of the Third Republic : not only in North Africa,
but in the Soudan and the Congo, in Madagascar and
Indo-China, have they endowed France with the second
greatest Colonial Empire in the world. Colonial power
has lain at the very root of the world war of 1914 ; the
settlement of colonial problems is bound to occupy more
than one clause in the future treaty of peace. Then it is,

B

when the German ambition of world-mastery is finally
disposed of, and when golden opportunities open to
peaceful enterprise, that the full value of the French
colonies, to France herself and to the world at large,
can be completely realised.   Even now, through the
ordeal of war, France is being supported to a greater
extent than she could expect by her colonies, who,
without being able to do as much for her as the great
British Dominions have done for this country, send her
not only food and raw materials, but some of her bravest
and most devoted soldiers—a great disappointment to
Germany, who had been for years glancing covetously
at the finest parts of the French Colonial Empire, and
had prepared everything for a rising of Islam against
French rule in Africa.   The conversation between Sir
Edward Goschen and the German Chancellor on
July 29, 1914, has not been forgotten.   I quote from the
Blue Book : " Provided that the neutrality of Great
Britain were certain (said Bethmann-Hollweg), every
assurance would be given to the British Government
that the Imperial Government aimed at no territorial
acquisitions at the expense of France. . . .   I questioned His Excellency about the French colonies, and
he said that he was unable to give a similar undertaking
in that respect."   After the war, Prévost Paradol's,
not Bethmann-Hollweg's dream, will be a reality.

The battle of the Marne, after the great retreat which
was the consequence of Charleroi and Mons, is only
one, and the most striking, illustration of how the
French can rally after a severe trial, how they can re-
trieve the effects of their misfortunes, or their mistakes.
The present Colonial Empire of the French is the

second they have held in the course of their history. The first had been built up by the labours of French explorers, missionaries and merchant adventurers in the seventeenth and eighteenth centuries : it included, in America, Eastern Canada and the whole Mississippi valley (then called Louisiana, after the name of the French king), and most of the Windward Islands with the great isle of San Domingo ; in Africa, settlements in the Senegal and in Madagascar, Bourbon and the Isle of France (now la Réunion and Mauritius); in Asia, the Dekkan Peninsula and Chandernagor in Bengal, with far-reaching connections in other parts of India. These were the promises of a magnificent Empire. But they were shattered by the naval and colonial victories of England in the Seven Years' War. Louis XV.'s government showed nothing but indifference : when Montcalm, the defender of French Canada, came to Versailles and begged for more troops, he was told in plain language, that " when the house is on fire it is not the time to bother about the stables." Public opinion was even more apathetic : Voltaire could not understand how highly civilised nations could be barbarous enough to fight for the possession of " a few acres of snow "—meaning Canada. So the foundations of a great world-empire were uprooted by the Treaty of Paris in 1763. What remained of the French colonies at the end of the eighteenth century was lost in consequence of the Napoleonic wars : in 1814, France recovered only a few of the smaller Antilles, the mouth of the Senegal river in Africa, la Réunion in the Indian Ocean and the Five Towns in India, mere relics of a great, irrecoverable past, the memory of which has

been kept alive to this day by the existence of the French-
speaking populations of Canada, the West Indies and
Mauritius.

The creation of the second Colonial Empire of
France was begun in 1830, when a French expedition-
ary force landed near Algiers. The government of the
day seems to have had nothing in view but to establish
its military prestige, to make the French people respect
the white flag of the restored monarchy, and forget the
tricolour. Whether they would have succeeded is open
to doubt, but, as a matter of fact, the Revolution of
July, 1830, put an end to both government and monarchy a few weeks after the French troops had entered
Algiers. The government that followed had for a long
time no settled policy in Algeria ; the French remained
there largely for the same reason which had sent their
first army across the Mediterranean ; King Louis
Philippe and his bourgeois ministers, just because they
wanted to maintain peace in Europe, thought they had
better keep the imagination of the French people occupied by stories of African campaigns. Only in the late
forties, something like a colonial policy began to evolve
out of what was originally a military display. About
the same time, French sailors occupied several islands
in the Pacific, including Tahiti and New Caledonia ;
they arrived just too late, if we are to believe the current
story, to hoist the French flag in New Zealand.

The Second Republic, after the Revolution of 1848,
was too short-lived and too deeply absorbed in internal
problems to take much interest in colonial enterprise.
Nevertheless, one very important landmark in the history of the French colonies bears the date of 1848 ; it

was the Republican government of 1848 who finally abolished slavery, after it had been suppressed for the first time by the Convention in 1783 and re-established by Napoleon. The name of the great Alsatian, Schelcher, who led the anti-slavery movement in France and moved the act of liberation, deserves to be remembered side by side with those of Wilberforce and Lincoln. The government of Napoleon III. made some fitful attempts at colonial expansion. Not to mention their ill-fated adventure in Mexico, they completed the conquest of Algeria, and tried there rather too many successive and conflicting systems of administration. They occupied Cochin-China in the Far East. The best piece of work done in the colonial field during that period was achieved in Senegal by General Faidherbe who, before he won undying fame by his masterly defence of Northern France in the latter part of the Franco-German War, had been, in our old West African colony, a wise, humane and far-seeing ruler. In spite of many blunders, the French establishment in North Africa was growing prosperous and deserved already to be thought of as an object of great expectations, and then it was that Prévost Paradol wrote the book I have mentioned. Arabs from Algeria fought, and fought well, in the ranks of the French army against the Germans in 1870.

It was one of the great works of national reconstruction undertaken after the disaster of 1870, to make France again what she was becoming in the eighteenth century, before the Seven Years' War began—a great colonial Power. An era of discovery and conquest was opening in Africa ; France had already a strong footing there, and her enterprises developed so successfully in the thirty years that followed, that she now rules one-third of the whole African continent. Her North African possessions were extended in 1881 by her protectorate over Tunis, and have been completed in 1912, after diplomatic incidents which need not be recalled, by her protectorate over Morocco. French West Africa (a huge territory, covering over 1,500,000 square miles) is the outcome of a series of explorations and expeditions in the eighties and nineties ; the first general agreement to determine the limits of the respective zones of influence of France and Great Britain in the Niger Valley was signed in 1890. In Equatorial Africa, French Congo is the creation of De Brazza, who, between 1875 and 1885, established by peaceful means French rule between the River Congo and the Atlantic coast ; the succession of enterprises, which were pushed northwards as far as Lake Tchad and the Central Soudan, took place between 1891 and 1900, and they found their limit in the East when Marchand, coming from the Atlantic, met Kitchener, marching up the Nile after the battle of Omdurman. The great island of Mada-gascar, where a treaty of protectorate had been signed as early as 1885, became finally a French colony after the expedition of 1894.

In Asia, Cochin-China had been in the possession of the French since 1862 ; after 1870, the pioneer work done by their explorers and merchants was followed by the conquest of Tonkin in 1885, the establishment of a French protectorate over Annam, and gradually by the control of the whole valley of the great Mekong river.

The piling up of so many names and dates may seem tiresome, but it is the only means of conveying in a few sentences the idea of what has been accomplished, in the course of a generation, by France after her ordeal of forty-eight years ago, when her enemies proclaimed that she was a decadent nation. The French themselves did not at first realise the greatness of their own efforts, and no man has been more reviled than the minister who presented to his country Tunis and Indo-China, Jules Ferry—the Tonkinese, as his political opponents nicknamed him—forgetting that thus it was that the Romans honoured their great conquerors.

France now possesses a colonial estate second only to the British Empire. Its total area amounts to 4,500,000 square miles, twenty times the size of France herself, and about the same as the whole of the British colonies and protectorates in Africa and Asia put together. Two million square miles at least can be successfully occupied and developed. The total population, including Morocco, is about 55,000,000 inhabitants, and the total trade in 1913 amounted to 3,250,000,000 francs (£130,000,000), equal to the foreign trade of Spain added to that of Italy, or to the nominal value of the imports and exports of the United States only forty years ago.

If we wish to realise the possibilities of the French Colonial Empire, and to see that they are now more than mere promises, let us remember what are the two main objects of colonial establishments. They may be, as the French put it, "colonies de peuplement," like Canada or New Zealand, or "colonies d'exploitation," like India or Nigeria. France has both, and has already had time to show that she knows how to make use of them.

Almost the only country, outside the British Dominions, in which a new community of white men can grow, is to be found in the French territories of North Africa, between the Atlantic and the Gulf of Gabes. Though divided into three parts under three separate administrations, it is geographically one country, the land of the Atlas mountains, and the fact that the Sahara Desert separates it from tropical Africa makes it practically an island. It belongs in fact to the Mediterranean world, and the very short distance from France (only twenty-four hours from Marseilles to Algiers) gives it a conspicuous advantage over all other colonies in the world.

The population of North Africa puts before the French administration a problem the like of which, I think, does not exist anywhere else ; but its satisfactory solution will open a great future to the North African community. In the British Dominions and colonies, you find either a society of white men in possession of the land which once belonged to a small and now decreasing native population, as in Canada or Australia, or practically no white settlers, as in India, because the climate does not allow the white race to live and thrive there. The only exception is South Africa, where a large and growing negro population is living side by side with British and Boer. But the situation in Algeria, Tunis and Morocco is quite different : there you have a native race (or rather two, the Arabs and the Berbers, mixed together and connected by the link of religion) who are not only growing rapidly in numbers, but

capable of a high civilisation. There can be no doubt
as to this when one thinks of what the Berbers had
become under the Roman rule—Saint Augustine was a
Berber—and of what the Arabs achieved in the Middle
Ages. And, under conditions of soil and climate very
similar to those found on the northern shores of the
Mediterranean, a white population is gathering and
becoming prosperous : a blend of French, Spanish,
Italian and Maltese blood, with the French language
and under French institutions, a genuine North African
society, imbued with the spirit of enterprise of a new
race on an almost virgin ground. The total population,
including Morocco, amounts to more than 12,000,000,
men of European descent being already 1,000,000.
How to harmonise the two elements and prepare them
for the brilliant future before them is a fascinating
problem.

The French began in Algeria, as most nations have
done in similar cases, by many more or less considered
experiments and by some notorious blunders. But time
and results have taught them. Algeria is at present one
of the most progressive countries round the Mediterranean. In Tunis we tried a system of protectorate,
which has been highly successful. M. Paul Cambon,
the distinguished French ambassador in London, who
had the opportunity and deserves the credit of setting
the machine going almost immediately after the conquest, can be proud of what Tunis has become. Such
a competent judge of colonial administration as Lord
Cromer used to say that he knew of no happier experiment than the one conducted by the French in
Tunis. Morocco has just come under French control,

and some of its mountains have been left untouched as yet; but a system very similar to that which has worked so well in Tunis is being gradually applied to Morocco by the very skilful and tactful, though very firm hand of our Resident, General Lyautey.

There is room in North Africa for a population as large as that of France herself. When all the available water (a most important consideration in a dry climate) is fully utilised and adequately distributed, when the methods of dry farming are understood and practised by the native farmer, there is no reason why North Africa, with its great wealth of minerals, iron, copper, zinc, petrol and phosphates, and its millions of sheep, which find on its extensive uplands conditions similar to those of the Australian plains, should not become one of the richest among the new countries of the Old World. It is, moreover, favoured by its geographical position, so near to Europe and on one of the main strategical and commercial routes of the globe. To have a vision of the country's future, it is enough to visit the great modern city of Algiers, in the heart of which are enshrined, as it were, the picturesque remains of the hilly capital of the Moorish pirates. It is enough to watch the growth of that city, which has now more than 170,000 inhabitants, and of its port, the traffic of which had tripled in the ten or twelve years before the war, and had become, in 1913, almost equal to that of Marseilles. It is the growth of North Africa, perhaps, more than any other factor, that will keep to France her rank among the great world-powers. Everywhere in North Africa the French find encouraging traces of a great precedent, that of the Romans. The *Roumis* of

Algiers try to follow the steps and hope to renew the gigantic work of Imperial Rome.

If, from the " colonies de peuplement," we now come to the " colonies d'exploitation," what are France's assets in that direction, and what is she doing with them at the present time ? In a recent speech, the Chancellor of the Exchequer was drawing the attention of Parliament to the importance of the supply of raw materials after the war, and warning Germany that the control of raw materials in a self-sufficing empire might be a powerful weapon against any nation who would not agree to terms securing a just and lasting peace. The French Colonial Empire, though it cannot in that respect be compared to the British Empire or to the United States, enables France to control very important supplies of essential articles.

She receives already, and will receive more and more in the future, foodstuffs from her colonies : during the war, her North African possessions, including Morocco, have sent her corn to the value of 70,000,000 francs in 1916 ; sheep nearly one million head in a year, for the consumption of the army ; Morocco sent to France, in 1916, 4,500,000 eggs. Great fisheries have been established on the coast of Mauritania, north of the Senegal river. Madagascar breeds a fine race of black cattle, and has a growing industry of tinned meat and frozen meat. I remember eating bully beef from Diego Suarez when I was in the ranks of the French Army, in the early months of the present war. Tonkin and Cochin-China produce rice in such quantities that they exported it in 1913 to the value of 176,000,000 francs (£7,000,000 sterling). It is from Indo-China that

France imported most of the rice required for her population ; unfortunately that importation has been made difficult by the shortage of shipping, and has been greatly reduced of late to save tonnage. The valley of the Niger, when properly irrigated and exploited, will also yield large quantities of rice, and is expected to become one of the greatest granaries of the world ; and there are large possibilities for sheep-breeding on the plateaux of the Atlas countries, as well as for cattle in the great plains of Central and Western Soudan. Kola, with its invigorating qualities, is practically a monopoly of West Africa.

West Africa is also the home of oil seeds, and the French possessions there, in 1913, exported £3,500,000 worth of pea-nuts, palm kernels, and palm oil. French Congo is part of the extensive rubber-producing area that covers a large part of the whole Congo basin ; it can also yield important supplies of all sorts of valuable wood. Madagascar, likewise, will some day be made rich by the production of rubber and wood. Raw materials for textiles are not at present supplied to any great extent by the French colonies, but the Western Soudan gives promise of becoming a great cotton-producing country. What has been said before as to the future of sheep-breeding in North Africa shows that France can also look forward to her colonies for supplying her market with wool.

Neither is the French Colonial Empire without mineral wealth. We have mentioned already the phosphates of Gafsa and Tebessa, the strata of which cover a considerable territory across Eastern Algeria and Southern Tunis. Their value amounts to hundreds of

millions, and their importance is at present emphasised
by the difficulties under which French agriculture has
been labouring during the war; the unwelcome deficiency
in the French crops is partly due to the lack of phosphates,
in consequence of the shipping situation. As for metals,
there are valuable deposits of iron ore in Algeria and
Tunis, mostly in the vicinity of the coast ; part of these
mines have been worked for a comparatively long time,
while some others, like those of the Ouenza district, con-
stitute great reserves for the near future. Iron has been
also found in Morocco, as well as copper, and there is
some in Madagascar. Nickel is found in great quantities
in New Caledonia, which is, with Canada, practically the
only country in the world to produce nickel ore. The
value of nickel exported from the island in 1913 exceeded
£4,000,000, and alongside with nickel there are deposits
of chrome and cobalt. Tin and wolfram, mixed together
as they very often are, have been discovered in Indo-
China. Tonkin has coal, of the same quality as Japanese
coal, with mines close to the sea, like the mines in Japan.
Coal from Madagascar is being used in that country and
in the neighbouring islands. Algeria has the privilege,
in a part of the world where coal is lacking and has to
be imported, to possess oil-fields which have just begun
to attract the attention of French and British capital.
The mineral wealth of the French colonies cannot be
measured by what they yield now ; though by no means
inconsiderable, the present output of their mines is
nothing to what it can and will be in the next few years.

Although France could certainly have achieved more,
if she had had more men to send to her colonies,
there was a remarkable development of colonial enter-

prise in the years immediately before the outbreak of war. Algeria and Tunis had had time to create a full system of roads and railways, which now begins to extend to Morocco. In West Africa an important programme of railway construction had been partly completed before 1914 : two lines running from the coast reached already the Niger river, while a third one from the Gulf of Guinea extended far into the Western Soudan. Indo-China was developing a complete network of railways which, from Tonkin, had been pushed far into the Chinese province of Yunnan. We should not forget great schemes of improvement, such as the irrigation of the Niger valley. War itself has not interrupted such a promising activity.

It is not surprising that Germany, to whom colonial ambition has occurred too late, and who was so pathetically complaining that she had not " her place in the sun," should have looked with covetous eyes upon the French colonies. As they did in various parts of the world, they approached them in two ways : the first one being for the time of peace, when they used the enterprising, if sometimes unscrupulous methods of their trade ; the second one, in view of a future war, consisting of an elaborate system of spying and a skilful preparation of risings among the native population. I might add a third : that of direct threats, such as they resorted to in the Moroccan negotiations.

A few concrete examples will illustrate this. In French Indo-China, ships under the German flag had steadily increased in number and tonnage, till in 1912 they came first on the list, after the French shipping. In the great Tonkinese harbour of Haiphong they did even better, the German tonnage having become as important there as the French and British tonnage put together. Two powerful German firms of general dealers had their hands in the imports and exports of the whole country as well as in the coastwise trade and the staple industry of rice. North Africa was being invaded by German goods, though in Morocco, where their actual commercial interests were never in proportion to their political claims, the figures for German trade did not show any increase in the last three years before the war. German capital was at the same time making great efforts to obtain the control of the new iron-mines in Algeria.

But, as if they had known that war was bound to come, the Germans were preparing another sort of conquest, by fostering an eventual rising of the Moors against France. There, as in the Near East, we now fully understand the real meaning of the theatrical declarations of friendship and protection repeatedly made by the Kaiser to the world of Islam. Sometimes the Germans went too far and indulged in clumsy demonstrations, such as the town of Algiers witnessed more than once. A flood of German tourists came every year to visit Algeria and Tunis, being as much as 70 per cent. of the total number of visitors; their attitude frequently called for attention, for they behaved as they would in a conquered territory, went about the streets after dinner singing the " Wacht am Rhein," and some of them openly declared to both Europeans and natives that the day was coming when the country would be theirs. Germany sent also to North Africa more discreet emissaries; scholars in the Arabic language visited the country and came into touch with the religious brotherhood ; one of them, pretending to have been converted to Islam and wearing the costume of the Arabs, was denounced by the natives themselves at the beginning of the war. When the war broke out, and especially after Turkey had joined in it, pamphlets and popular songs were circulated heralding the triumph of the Germans and the coming of El Hadj Guilioun, the Friend of the Faithful ! In Morocco, everything had been planned for arming the populations and throwing the French into the sea, and, after this had failed, the existence of the Spanish zone enabled German agents, and local chiefs in the pay of Germany, to continue their underground work.

But what have been the results ? In Algeria there have been only two small incidents, the most important of which was, in October, 1914, the riot of the Beni Chougran, occasioned by recruiting operations. The trouble there was limited to an inconsiderable area and was stopped almost immediately. In Morocco, the situation might have been much more dangerous. The country had been occupied only recently, and its occupation was still incomplete. When the French Government thought that war was inevitable they sent a dispatch to General Lyautey, requiring him to send to France the greater part of the troops under his command, and, as the remaining forces would not be sufficient to garrison the whole country, he was instructed to abandon temporarily all but the coast-line, which reduced the occupation of Morocco to that of a few seaports. But General Lyautey took a bold decision, as a soldier and a statesman would : since France received

all the men she required, was it not for him to decide
whether he could hold his positions or not ? He felt
certain that if he evacuated his outstanding forts, not
to speak of the large towns, the whole population would
rise. So he stood firm, sent most of his troops to France,
and, with a mere handful of men, he faced the danger,
and kept the whole of Morocco. The natives were im-
pressed when they saw all our male civilians in uniform,
and said : " We did not know that all the French were
soldiers in disguise." Later on, General Lyautey
received reinforcements and could easily hold his own.
While, by a continuous marching and counter-marching
of his small forces, and well-prepared expeditions on a
limited scale, he actually increased the area under
French rule, and surrounded in their mountains the
independent tribes, he took great care to impress the
population by his apparent unconcern with the European
war, undertaking public works, building hundreds of
miles of roads and military railways, organising ex-
hibitions to which even natives from the unconquered
parts flocked by thousands. What has happened in
Morocco is a striking instance of how France retained
her hold on her subject populations during the war.

The colonies have done more than remain quiet and
loyal : they have been of the greatest assistance to
France in her struggle. Algeria alone has sent to France
100,000 European and 120,000 native soldiers. The
native population is now liable to conscription, by the
old French system of the drawing of lots : they readily
submit to it, and separation allowances are not only
popular but revolutionise the native society by putting,
for the first time since many centuries, money into the

c

hands of the native wife. A Moroccan division won glory early in the campaign, by the bravery of its Moorish soldiers. The colonies also send labour to France : Kabyles are working in foundries and munition works, and a number of them can be seen cleaning the streets of Paris. Annamites, with their delicate hands, make themselves useful in hospitals. This is the first time that the populations of the various parts of the French Colonial Empire have had so many opportunities to come into contact with France herself, and this will certainly tend to create permanently a closer connection between them and the French nation.

Into the great society of the Allies, which, no one of us doubts, will survive, France does not enter alone. She is surrounded by the new countries for the future of which she is responsible. What she can and will do with them will largely decide her own future. The spirit the nation has shown, not only on the battlefields, but in the creation and management of war industries, demonstrates that, apart from the heroic deeds of her soldiers, she is capable of steady and organised efforts. Such efforts will be continued after the war ; many traditions of timidity and procrastination will have been swept away. The need for bold enterprise will be found everywhere and promise great rewards. Then it is that all the reserves of strength and wealth, which the French colonies keep for France and for the world, will be thrown into the scale where sinks and rises the greatness of nations.

CHAPTER III

THE COLONIAL ASPIRATIONS OF GERMANY

By J. E. MACKENZIE, B.A.
Formerly Berlin Correspondent of *The Times*

COLONISATION is in German a word of somewhat peculiar significance. As has often been said, the German people is itself essentially, and to a larger degree than most other peoples, a *Kolonisations-Volk*. It was by colonisation that it spread, for instance, over German Austria, Saxony, Silesia, Mecklenburg and large parts of Prussia itself. The Prussians are still " colonists " in Poland, in Schleswig-Holstein, in Alsace-Lorraine ; and when we speak of their " colonial " aspirations it would be tempting enough to follow them into Flanders and into Courland and Lithuania. Where, again, is the line to be drawn between " colonisation " and the organised " penetration " of foreign countries ? And ought we to consider the peculiar determination with which the Germans have organised, and are now trying to reorganise, their control of what they call *Auslandsdeutschtum*— Germanism abroad ?

In reality, of course, I must confine myself to oversea possessions—possessions held before the war and now lost, or possessions which Germany yet hopes to recover or to obtain. But the distinction is, in a sense, arbitrary. The real problem is the problem of the outward pressure of Germany upon the world. That

pressure may be exerted, first, by annexation or domination on the Continent of Europe ; secondly, by what
is called " penetration " of foreign countries ; and,
thirdly, by the seizure, purchase, or other acquisition,
of overseas possessions. Best of all, if the three methods
can be combined ! But it is, perhaps, " penetration "
which is most of all desired by modern German
diplomacy.

There, however, I must leave both the sort of
" colonisation " which is being practised by the Germans in Flanders and the Baltic Provinces, and which
one could study before the war at Strassburg, or in
Prussian Poland ; and also the sort of " colonisation "
which has been scotched, but hardly as yet killed, in the
United States, Central and South America, the Far East,
or, to come nearer home, in Manchester and London.

When the present German Empire was united by
blood and iron through the successful wars of 1864,
1866 and 1870, no German State possessed a foot of
territory outside the Continent of Europe. Only thirty-
five years have passed since Herr Adolf Lüderitz, a
Bremen merchant, obtained the grudging promise of
government protection for the acquisition of a small
stretch of land on the coast of South-West Africa.
Most of us are probably familiar with the main outline
of subsequent events. So far as this country was concerned, our statesmen showed neither great vigilance
nor conspicuous foresight. So far from taking advantage of Bismarck's reluctance to embark upon any
colonial policy whatever, we made hesitating objections
which we were not prepared to uphold, and which only

helped the German adventurers to overcome the scruples of the German Foreign Office and the opposition of the German Reichstag. In a period of about eighteen months Germany was firmly established in Africa. On April 24, 1884, Bismarck sent his famous telegram to the German Consul at Cape Town, announcing that the Lüderitz concessions were under German protection. Very soon afterwards Mr. Gladstone pronounced his equally famous blessing in the House of Commons : " If Germany is to become a colonising Power, all I say is, God speed her. She becomes our ally and partner in the great purposes of Providence for the advantage of mankind."

The Germans acted with great rapidity. In the course of the year 1884 Herr Nachtigal, the German Consul-General at Tunis, acquired both Togo and German Cameroon, and Karl Peters began the conquest of German East Africa. In the same year, 1884, Germany stretched out her arm over the Pacific. Before the end of 1885 she had acquired Kaiser Wilhelmsland (the northern part of New Guinea), the Bismarck Archipelago, part of the Solomon Islands, the Marschall Islands and the Carolines. In 1897 she seized Kiao-Chau. In 1899 she obtained Samoa. Thus Germany had suddenly become the third greatest colonial Power of the world, and held colonial territory five times the extent of the German Empire.

I have made the inevitable—and superficial—criticism of British policy in 1884 and the following years. But it is a mistake to suppose that we then suffered merely from the blindness of peculiar statesmen, who were incapable of penetrating the motives and meanings of German intrigue. All policy is governed to some extent by temporary circumstances. We were ignorant, no doubt. But our real ignorance at that time was not so much ignorance of Germany and of coming events in Europe, as ignorance of the British Empire, not so much under-estimation of the immense power of German unity as under-estimation of the immense possibilities of British—we can now at last say Anglo-Saxon—cohesion. And so now we have not merely to repair the mistakes of thirty years ago, but, profiting by our mistakes, to rebuild our whole policy upon the sure foundation of our ideals. Let us not distort history, as the Germans do. They, so far as I can judge them, are busily establishing the doctrine that Bismarck, when he resisted the colonial adventurers because he needed peace in Europe, had become senile and short-sighted. When the East African escapade was at its height Bismarck formally instructed Herr von Holstein, who may be called the " hidden hand " in the German Foreign Office of that time, that the maintenance of Lord Salisbury in office was worth more than all Witu ; and he wrote in his chief newspaper that " the existing friendship with England is for us of greater value than all that the expedition on the Upper Nile could in the most favourable event achieve." As late as 1894, Caprivi, Bismarck's successor, said that the Germans should " thank God, if nobody offered them the whole of Africa." Were Bismarck and Caprivi really wrong ?

I cannot, however, deal further here with the beginnings of the German Colonial Empire. The subject will repay study. Indeed, there are few chapters in the history of the world at once so important, so small in compass, so complete in themselves, and so rich in political lessons. A whole overseas Empire won and lost within a single generation !

There is one point to which attention may be called, the extreme difficulty of determining in advance the actual political consequences of territorial changes. My own slight experience as an onlooker at international negotiations leads me to think that the negotiators seldom, if ever, have their attention fixed upon the immediate material of the negotiation. Think of the part which Morocco has played in the history of the past ten years. Or the Baghdad Railway. Or the Balkans. Or the Belgian Congo. Such questions arise suddenly, from some single initiative or concatenation of international circumstances. There usually follows what is called a " crisis," and thenceforward the real question is whether the crisis can be solved peacefully or not. It is not the experts on the particular question who usually determine the ultimate issue, and so it is not surprising that those who do decide the issue are seldom right in their estimate of the practical consequence of what they are doing. As regards the building up of the German Colonial Empire, the classical case of leaping in the dark is the acquisition of Heligoland. That island, which now looms so large in our view of the naval war, was ceded to Germany in 1890 in exchange for the abandonment of the German protectorate over the Witu coast and the final recognition of the British protectorate over Zanzibar. The bargain is commonly regarded as a terrible proof of somnolence on the part of Lord Salisbury and of cunning on the part of Germany, and the Kaiser has twice at least during the war claimed credit for his omniscient foresight in this matter in the first years of his reign. But the truth appears to be that the bargain was not really understood on either side. In Germany the supposed surrender of Zanzibar—to which, as a matter of fact, Germany had no claim—produced a violent explosion of Pan-German fury—and until quite a short time before the war Heligoland was regarded by many otherwise well-informed Englishmen as a crumbling rock, upon the attempted fortification of which Germany was spending large sums which she could very ill afford. In almost any German book written before the war you will find it taken for granted that Germany had much the worst of the bargain.

Professor Andler, of the Sorbonne, has said in his valuable volume on *Colonial Pan-Germanism* that the original reasons for German colonial ambitions were prestige and sentiment. That is perfectly true. The more prosaic explanations were discovered and put forward *afterwards*. A particularly daring propaganda, which still, I am afraid, lives on in many quarters even in England, developed the fiction that Germany possessed a large " surplus population " which must find an " outlet." The quite temporary phenomena of abnormal emigrations were exploited in this sense, and credulous foreign countries and foreign governments were induced to believe that Germany, shut in on all sides, was faced by the tragic fate of seeing her growing peoples drift away under foreign flags, because they had nowhere else to go. Germany never had a surplus popu-

lation ; what she had for a time was a population which
was increasing at an increasing rate ; and the settlement
and employment of this population were rendered pre-
carious by economic changes, and especially by the
economic convulsions in Germany itself. Germany was
ceasing to be mainly agrarian and becoming largely
industrial, with the result that the economic equilibrium
of the country was disturbed. For many years Germany
has had a population which is increasing at a steadily
decreasing rate—the downward progress being partly
obscured by the combating of infant mortality and
other improvements of public health. On the other
hand, she has had to fear that her large *importation* of
foreign labour would be threatened when her neighbours
were strong enough to resist her commercial dictation.
This question of imported labour was becoming ex-
tremely urgent as between Germany and Russia, and it
was an important factor in the Prussian decision to
" have things out " with Russia in 1914. But I need
not labour this question of population. In 1911, when
the last Morocco crisis had produced a fresh outburst
of chauvinism, Count Posadowsky, the former Minister
of the Interior, who was, I think, the ablest German
statesman of his time, exposed the " surplus population " myth in public, and pointed out that Germany
had to import hundreds of thousands of foreigners—he
might have said at least a million—to till German soil
and work German mines. In reality every German
writer of any standing has abandoned the population
myth. There is now but one survival of the belief that
Germany needs colonies for *settlement*—a curious doctrine that colonies might absorb some of the excessive

output of the German high schools and universities. Thus Professor Hans Delbrück complains that, while the only " educated " classes which Germany imported before the war were jockeys, dancing-masters, teachers of languages and children's nurses, she was exporting her precious chemists, engineers and trained workmen ; he would now like to see the latter establishing themselves in " an overseas Germany " as the bearers of *Kultur* and the lords and educators of lower races.[1] Meanwhile we may note that, on the most liberal computation, the whole white population of the German colonies never exceeded 20,000. They formed, alas ! but a tiny fraction of the countless number of African natives who have been exterminated by German wars and German administration.

As it is sometimes argued that, although Germany has no colonists now, she may have them later on, I should add that, in point of fact, she not only demands that Russians, Poles and various races of the Austro-Hungarian Empire shall supply her with migratory farm-labour and miners ; but it is of the utmost importance to her shipping that she should keep control of emigration from the European hinterland. Hamburg lives by emigration, but it is emigration not from Germany but from Poland and Galicia. That is why she fights bitterly any non-German shipping enterprise based, for example, upon Trieste. I must not wander too far into what the Germans call *Weltwirtschaft*—world-economics. But when we talk of the colonial developments of the future, we should remember that the whole world is in convulsion, and that

---

[1] *Bismarcks Erbe*, von Hans Delbrück, 1915, p. 195.

many economic currents, including the migrations of human labour and enterprise, will assuredly flow in directions other than those with which we have been familiar. They are also likely to flow in directions other than those which we foresee.

As we have seen, German colonial policy was launched some years before the accession of the Emperor William II. For many years the only result was disappointment and depression. Bismarck had occasional fits of enthusiasm. But Bismarck would not depart from his view that the flag should follow trade, not trade follow the flag. The policy of private ventures and chartered companies was a hopeless failure. German opinion was lukewarm or positively cold. The German expeditions were a mixture of vague Imperialist sentiment and petty commercialism. The German colonial pioneers were, for the most part, as defective in moral character as in statesmanship. A great deal of valuable work was done by German explorers, geographers, anthropologists, and philologists. But the achievements of Prussian militarism in Africa culminated in the bloody and disgraceful war against the Hereros ; the achievements of German adminis-tration in the " colonial scandals " which came to a head in 1906. All this is fully admitted by German historians. " Our ultimate and real mistake," says Professor Delbrück in a book published in 1915, " was that we had engaged upon colonisation, not as a great political act, but partly from obscure national impulses, and partly in the belief that we were engaged in purely economic action—in business." [1]

[1] Delbrück, *op. cit.*, p. 187.

The outlook in the colonial sphere was, indeed, as bad as it could be. What changed the situation was the rapid development of a new foreign policy under William II., and, above all, the construction of the German Navy and the proclamation that Germany's future lay upon the water. Henceforward German colonial policy was to be an essential part of German world-policy, and, especially, to be the sister of German naval policy. For a time it might seem that naval expansion competed with colonial expansion, naval expenditure with colonial expenditure. But "the new course" of William and Prince Bülow was, in the long run, certain to produce a powerful colonial movement, and to employ the hitherto unprofitable overseas possessions as political bases.

We well remember the series of electric shocks which Germany administered to the world in the years which followed the outbreak of the South African War—the great Navy Bill of 1900 ; the first Morocco crisis ; the pounce upon Turkey and prosecution of the scheme to descend by the Baghdad Railway upon the Persian Gulf ; the intrigues in Russia, upon which so much new light has lately been shed ; the use made of the Venezuela crisis. Meanwhile the colonial movement seemed to languish. Suddenly, at the end of 1906, the Kaiser and Bülow made the colonies the great test question of Imperialism. After the exposure of the "colonial scandals" the Reichstag had thrown out a colonial railway vote. Prince Bülow sprang up and read the Emperor's order dissolving the Reichstag ; he had it ready in his pocket. He had already dismissed Prince Ernest Hohenlohe, the rather insignificant head of the

Colonial Department of the Foreign Office, and
appointed as his successor Herr Bernhard Dernburg.
Dernburg, an ambitious Jewish banker, who had been
trained in the United States, ran a highly successful
election campaign on lines hitherto unknown in Germany. For one of his principal meetings he mobilised
the whole teaching staff of Berlin University. They
issued a public appeal, which I preserved as a memento
of the elections, and it admirably illustrates the nature
of the movement. The Berlin professors said :

" The policy which has given our Fatherland such
important overseas interests, appears, in the light of
science and of history, not as a consequence of personal
inclinations [*i.e.* of the Kaiser] and the fancies of leading
statesmen [*i.e.* Bülow], but as one result of the development of German national consciousness and German
national economics, of German trade, German shipping,
German exports. Similar world-political tendencies
have arisen in all large and developed States in Europe
and America.

" The German people, which is only gradually growing up to this situation, must be taught that there can
no longer be any thought of abandoning our position
of world-power, and our colonies in particular, unless
the German people wants to abandon itself. Be one's
views about particular questions of world-policy what
they will, the world-political tendency in our State
policy can nevermore be checked."

One immediate result of the movement of 1906-7
was the removal of colonial administration from the
Foreign Office, and the establishment of a Colonial
Office with Dernburg as Colonial Secretary. We are

not concerned now with the history of his administration. He effected considerable reforms. But his gift for self-advertisement was not the least of his talents. I trust that opinion in England, upon which Dernburg imposed with some success, has not failed to discover that the real Dernburg is the Dernburg who in 1914 emerged from a retirement in which German opinion had been well content to leave him since 1910, and went to the United States on the mission—a Red Cross mission it was called—which ended in his expulsion. Let him be remembered for the service which he has involuntarily rendered in promoting the intervention of the United States.

The one important point to note about the period inaugurated by Dernburg in 1907 is that the avowed aims of German colonial administration became more and more definitely economic. The " surplus population " myth disappeared, or was retained only by German propagandists abroad, and in its place arose the doctrine that German overseas possessions must be made to overflow with German supplies. Colonisation was to be exploitation. It might or might not be accompanied by good and beneficial administration ; the treatment of natives might be good or bad. But the fundamental object was to be economic. The well-known German explorer of Cameroon, Herr Zintgraff, said in his time, with a wonderful flash of candour : " Africa for the Africans, but the Africans for us ! " Professor Moritz Bonn, of Munich—I quote him because he is a thoroughly representative authority who was well known in England before the war—said in 1911 : " The most important colony for Germany is not the colony which has the largest white population, but the colony which will produce continuously the largest quantities of raw materials and food stuffs which we require." [1] Such were at any rate the *avowed* aims. They certainly were strongly *futurist*. The statistics of German importation of colonial products are even more insignificant than the statistics of German emigration to the colonies. In fact, the trade argument is no more satisfactory than the population argument as evidence of the German need of overseas possessions. Germany's whole trade with her colonies in 1913 was—what do you suppose? Just one-half of one per cent. of her whole foreign trade !

In reality we must always come back to *Welt-politik*. German colonial aspirations are entirely contained in German world-ambitions. They can be understood—and judged—only in terms of general foreign policy, of Germany's place in the world, and of the hopes and plans of the non-German peoples. What are Germany's principal aims? First and foremost, the acquisition of a large, interconnected, self-contained block of territory in Africa. Herr Solf, the late Colonial Secretary, said in June, 1917, that his programme is " clear and simple." He declared himself against any " militarisation of Africa," but said : " We mean to have our colonial possessions back, and we want, as far as possible, so to shape them that they shall form a territory capable of resistance and of economic progress. . . . I should like to say that, before the war, and this in the clear recognition of the importance of contiguous colonial

[1] Bonn : *Die Neugestaltung unserer Kolonialen Aufgaben*, 1911.

possessions for the safe existence of the German nation, we had made far-reaching preparations in order that by peaceful understanding and agreement we might shape our colonial possessions in a way corresponding to the most urgent colonial necessities. . . . For a long time," he continued, "it had been even in England an open secret that even before the war we had plans for making a united whole of our African possessions by means of peaceful agreements." Upon this Herr Solf proceeded to denounce General Smuts and other British statesmen in whose speeches he discovered "a firm desire to annihilate Germany as a colonial power."

Just note this argument : it is characteristic. Because the British Government endeavoured to satisfy German aspirations in Africa before the war, it is a deadly sin for British statesmen and British public opinion to adopt a different attitude now. Many Germans—including Herr Solf—have used in the same way the blessings poured out by Gladstone and others on the early German colonies. How wicked the British nation must be, since it has wandered so far from the light ! Surely the truth is on the other side. The goodwill which we showed to the German Colonial Empire stands to *our* credit and not to the credit of Germany ; if our policy towards German colonial aims has been reversed, it has been through no fault of ours.

Herr Solf says that it is an open secret in England that Germany before the war had plans for making a united whole of her African possessions by means of peaceful agreements. After the Agadir crisis and the Franco-German Morocco Treaty of November, 1911, there was a considerable Anglo-German *détente*. There

was a regular European Concert during the Balkan
Wars ; there were the large naval and other negotiations connected with the name of Lord Haldane ; and,
above all, there were fruitful negotiations concerning
Asiatic Turkey and the Baghdad Railway on the one
hand, and concerning Africa on the other hand. The
existence of the agreements about " the Baghdad Railway and some kindred matters " was announced to the
House of Commons by Viscount Grey on June 29,
1914, but nothing was said in public before the outbreak of war about the African agreement. June 29
was the day after the murder of the Archduke Francis
Ferdinand ; at the time that Lord Grey was speaking I was travelling back from Kiel Regatta to Berlin in
the somewhat melancholy company of the German
Ambassador in London, Prince Lichnowsky. He told
me then that he was confident that the last difficulties
in the matter of the African agreement would be overcome. Five weeks later we were at war.[1]

I suppose it is now universally agreed that all the
Anglo-German negotiations of 1912-14 were futile,
and future historians will class them with those futile
proposals for disarmament with which British statesmanship occupied itself, much to the amusement of
Bismarck, on the very eve of the Franco-German
War of 1870.

I will not attempt to explore Herr Solf's " open

[1] Since this lecture was delivered Prince Lichnowsky's own account
of the African treaty and of the reasons why it was never signed has
become available by the disclosure of his memorandum, " My London
Mission." But it is not necessary to expand my reference to the matter,
which I mention only in tracing the character and sequence of German
aims.—J. E. M.

D

secret " as regards the actual agreements that were in contemplation. But there is certainly not much secret about what Germany was aiming at—and is still aiming at. As a matter of fact, the whole project may be studied in a pamphlet which was published anonymously in Berlin in 1913, under the title " German World-Policy and No War." The precise authorship is uncertain, but it may well have been the joint work of the German Colonial Office and the German Embassy in London. The interconnection of colonial aims with foreign policy was to be this, that, if German expansion were directed against Russia or France, that would consolidate the Triple Entente ; but, if Germany concentrated upon overseas expansion, British interference in continental questions need not be feared. Where could Germany find a field of overseas expansion which would not obviously collide with vital British interests ? Hitherto Germany had pursued her ambitions in every quarter of the globe. Why not concentrate on Africa ? And why not concentrate especially on the Belgian Congo and on the Portuguese colonies ? Germany hoped to acquire the right of pre-emption of the Belgian Congo in this way. France had in 1911 agreed not to exercise her right of pre-emption without reference to the signatory powers of the Berlin Treaty of 1885 ; England, if the question was raised, was to be attracted to Germany's side. Similarly, agreements with England were to make the Portuguese colonies an acknowledged German sphere of interests. There were to be no immediate annexations ; but when the fruit was ripe it was to fall into Germany's lap. In reality, of course, the ripening of the fruit would have been forced. The

main lever was admittedly to be the development of
railways. German "assistance" was to be pressed upon
Portugal, and the pressure could easily be supported
at Lisbon by forms of German diplomacy with which
we are all more familiar now than we were in 1914.
As regards the Belgian colonies, we now have very
definite evidence. We now know that in the spring of
1914 the German Foreign Secretary, Herr von Jagow,
made overtures to the French Ambassador in Berlin
for the purpose of Herr Solf's negotiations. He quite
candidly developed the theme that Belgium had too
heavy a colonial load on her shoulders and must be
relieved of it. "Only the Great Powers," he observed,
"were in a position to colonise," and the small States
were doomed either to disappear or to gravitate into
the orbits of the Great Powers. Finally, every one will
remember how, when the German Imperial Chancellor
tried to secure British neutrality by an assurance that
Germany "aimed at no territorial acquisitions at the
expense of France," Sir Edward Goschen questioned
him about the French colonies, and the Chancellor " said
that he was unable to give a similar undertaking in that
respect." The British Ambassador's intuition was perfectly sound. I imagine that the thought which flashed
through Herr von Bethmann-Hollweg's mind at that
strange midnight meeting was this : " You realise,
then, that the whole German policy of the last three
years, during which we have sought to secure British
neutrality, was to bring us our reward in the French
colonies as well as in the Portuguese colonies and in the
Belgian Congo." In this connection it should, further,
be noted that, while Germany was making effusive

promises about the ultimate integrity of Belgium, and even declared that it was impossible for her to annex Belgian territory without annexing Dutch territory also, she never gave any assurances whatever about the Belgian Congo.[1]

Put briefly, the German aim before the war was the creation, step by step, of a Colonial Empire—what Herr Solf calls "a united whole"—stretching right across Africa, linking German East Africa through the Belgian Congo with a much enlarged German Cameroon and running down through Angola to an enlarged German South-West Africa. That is the great aim now. It is avowed with ever-increasing candour ; its attractions are displayed in changing lights with the changing fortunes of war. At one moment "Central Africa" is linked up with "Central Europe"; that depends upon the destinies of Italy and the whole future of the Adriatic and the Ægean. At another moment "Central Africa" is linked up with Asia Minor, or even becomes the connecting link between the Atlantic and the Pacific; that depends upon the destinies of the Ottoman

[1] This statement in my lecture led to inquiry concerning the text of the German ultimatum which was presented to the Belgian Government on August 2, 1914. It was then seen that the French text, hastily prepared at Brussels, contains a serious mistranslation. Germany, in the event of Belgium maintaining neutrality, promised, at the conclusion of peace, "to guarantee in the fullest extent the territorial integrity and independence of Belgium (*Besitzstand und Unabhängigkeit des Königreichs in vollem Umfang zu garantieren*)." This language deliberately excluded a guarantee of the Belgian colonies, but was inaccurately translated "à garantir le royaume et ses possessions dans toute leur étendue," which, again, was translated into English " to guarantee the possessions and independence of the Belgian Kingdom in full."—J. E. M.

Empire. At yet another moment " Central Africa " is the natural base for German penetration of South and Central America. Two factors, however, are constant. The new Colonial Empire is to be self-contained and impregnable, so that no Power engaged in war in Europe will assail it. And it is to be a centre of German *naval* power, a *strategic* position, which, whether Africa is " militarised " or not, will affect every conceivable combination of forces, alter every problem of defence. There is to be a new Germany, based upon the open sea, and then the naval issue can no longer lie in the North Sea or the Baltic or the Mediterranean.

I have spoken almost entirely of Africa. Positive German aims are concentrated there. The German Government published in 1917 a formal announcement that it will not abandon the lost possessions in the Pacific, and from time to time it is indicated that Germany maintains her claim to Kiao-Chau. But there can be little doubt that she hopes to approach these problems in other ways than by the claim to Eastern territory. It is impossible in the scope of this paper to dissect all the strategic arguments, but let me quote a single plain statement ; it is by Herr Emil Zimmermann, the most eloquent exponent of the " Central Africa " policy. He writes :

" It is England—Japan apart—that is mainly responsible for our present evil situation in the Far East. The chief opponent of our expansion in the Pacific is Australia. Now, we can never exert pressure upon Australia from the South Seas ; but we can very well do it from East Africa. Australia needs for her exports an open road through the Indian Ocean. This road can be most seriously menaced from East Africa. Of course Australian trade can take the road round South Africa; but even on this route freight ships would not be safe against attacks from East Africa. Thus the policy of Australia and also of India could be most powerfully influenced. For England has just as great an interest in uninterrupted traffic with India and Australia as they have in uninterrupted traffic with England. When we have a position of power in Central Africa, with which India and Australia will have to reckon, we shall be able to force them both to respect our wishes in the South Seas and in the Far East, and so we shall drive the first wedge into the united front of our Far Eastern enemies."[1]

Meanwhile Germany has had many bitter disappointments. The part played by Australia and New Zealand in the war, the policy of Japan, the improvement in the relations of Japan and the United States, the expulsion of Germany from China, the ridicule provoked by her fantastic offer of an alliance with Japan through Mexico—all has gone very ill, and there is nothing to do but to wait and pray that chinks may appear in the armour of the vast coalition. Germany clamoured for world-policy; she has got it with a vengeance.

As I have said, German colonial policy has always been only one side of her world-policy. It is, I believe, —and I, for my part, most earnestly hope—too late for her to extricate her colonial aims from the wreck of other ambitions, too late for her to reconstruct any so-called " colonial " scheme which will wear, in the eyes of a now somewhat suspicious world, the appearance of a German contribution to peace.

[1] *Europäische Staats- und Wirtschafts-Zeitung*, June 23, 1917.

CHAPTER IV

THE MONROE DOCTRINE AND ITS TRANSFORMATION

By PROF. A. F. POLLARD, M.A., Litt.D.
Professor of English History in the University of London

" SOME men are born great, some achieve greatness,
and some have greatness thrust upon them." The
eponymous hero of the Monroe Doctrine belonged
rather to the third of these categories than to the first
or the second. The son of a Virginian planter, he was
certainly not born great ; and although he served in the
American War of Independence, was sent as envoy to
France in 1797 and 1803, and was twice elected President of the United States, no one would say that he
achieved measurable distance of the greatness of Presi-
dents like Washington, Lincoln, or Wilson. His fame
has come to him not for any personal qualities or
achievements, but rather from his more or less acci-
dental connection with a political doctrine which was
fashioned out of the circumstances and the mind of the
American people, and came to express vaguely and
varyingly their outlook upon external politics. It was
adumbrated rather than defined in Monroe's presidential message read to Congress on December 2, 1823 ;
but its authorship has been attributed to other minds
than that of the President himself, and it bears that
stamp of compromise which lends itself to various
interpretations.

Monroe himself was a man of kindly temperament rather than decisive intellect, and, despite the name the doctrine bears, it is popularly fathered upon more clear-cut personalities, Canning on this side of the Atlantic, John Quincy Adams on the other. There are other claimants for whom historical research might make out a plausible title, and as early as 1814 the Russian ambassador, Nesselrode, wrote to his master, the Emperor Alexander, that " the dominant party in America . . . is aiming at a complete revolution in the relations of the New World with the Old by the destruction of all European interests in the American continent." This quotation will serve to indicate the extent to which ideas subsequently associated with the Monroe Doctrine had permeated the American mind before Monroe himself had even entered upon his first term of presidential office. It indicates that the Monroe Doctrine, like most historical ideas and institutions, grew out of circumstances which turned many minds in the same direction, and was not conceived of sudden impulse or made by a single act of creation. It was the offspring not of a man but of a generation, and it grew out of the situation in which the people of the United States found themselves in face of the European Restoration after Napoleon's fall.

A similar declaration of political faith might have been precipitated even earlier, had Napoleon succeeded and had Great Britain disappeared as a buffer between the mighty Emperor of the Old World and the infant Hercules of the New. Saved from that menace, which only took occasional form in Napoleon's words, the United States could afford to resent the British blockade and to cherish the inherited conviction that George III. was a greater danger to democracy in America than Napoleon himself. At any rate the conflict between the two giants of the Old World promised respite, if not safety, for the New, and probably assisted the growth of a determination in America to preclude a similar contest between Legitimism and Revolution on its side of the Atlantic. But the Restoration made the danger greater if it did not bring it nearer. Legitimism came into its own again in Europe, but its own was not confined to Europe. The War of Liberation against Napoleon inured to the benefit of Bourbons, of Hapsburgs, and of Hohenzollerns; and although Great Britain refused to subscribe to the Holy Alliance, its association in the Quintuple Alliance with the three autocratic signatories to that document was enough to give it a shady complexion in the eyes of distant observers, and to arouse American apprehension of a Europe solidly wedded to the principles of Legitimism and Reaction. After all there still sat on the British throne the king who had fought a seven years' war to prevent the birth of republican freedom in America.

Nor was the danger precluded by the Atlantic Ocean; for nine-tenths of the American continents were still ruled or claimed as dominions by European monarchs, and the enunciation of the Monroe Doctrine was precipitated by the struggle between the Bourbon king of Spain and the vast possessions in North and South America which had come down to him from the days of Philip II. The opportunity for their revolt had been provided in 1807 by Napoleon's ejection of the Bourbon from the Spanish throne and the substitution of his

brother, Joseph Bonaparte ; and the success of this
liberation was facilitated by the British fleet, which
controlled the sea and prevented European intervention in the South American Wars of Independence.
The struggles, however, were long, and the issue was
still in doubt when the fall of the Napoleonic dynasts
and the restoration of the Bourbons in Europe produced fresh complications. As between the Bonapartes and the revolted Spanish colonies our British
attitude was clear enough ; but the re-established
Bourbons were our allies, and while sympathy with the
colonists remained, overt action on their behalf became a
delicate matter. Spain herself was divided in opinion ; a
Liberal but impracticable Constitution had been set up
in 1812 to the accompaniment of Wellington's march
and the rising of Spain against the Bonapartes. The
restored Bourbons had, however, little love for Consti-
tutions, and Ferdinand VII. was equally bent on re-
establishing autocracy in Spain and on recovering the
Spanish colonies. Fortunately, perhaps, he was a feeble
king who failed in the preliminary operation of restoring
his authority at home. But his Liberal ministers were
hardly less incompetent, and the Constitution they
endeavoured to enforce produced an anarchy which
invited intervention by the brother Bourbon across the
Pyrenees. It was one of the points of the Holy Alliance
that kings were a band of brothers bound to render
each other assistance against insurgent subjects. England was no party to that pact, and refused at the
Congress of Verona to countenance joint action for this
purpose. France, however, went on, with the blessings
of Russia, Austria and Prussia. The Duke of Angou-

lême crossed the Pyrenees in April, 1823. Spain failed
to repeat against the Bourbons the history of her up-
rising against the Bonapartes ; Madrid was occupied
by French troops in July, Ferdinand was re-seated
on his autocratic throne, and by the end of Sep-
tember Cadiz alone upheld the cause of the Liberal
Constitution.

Louis XVIII. had apparently succeeded where
Louis XIV. had failed, and the Pyrenees had been
abolished in the interests of reaction and the Bourbons.
The English mind was switched back from the Napoleonic wars to those of the Spanish Succession, from
the needs of the Restoration to the fear of the Bourbon
pacte de famille. But she could no longer look for
assistance to the Hapsburgs, for Hapsburg and Bourbon
were at one with each other as well as with Hohenzollerns and Romanoffs in their devotion to the Legi-
timist cause ; and Spain at least was lost. But if the
Pyrenees had disappeared, Canning was resolved to
maintain the Atlantic Ocean. Spain might be lost, but
her colonies might be saved ; the Old World might
surrender to reaction, the New might be preserved for
progress. As Angoulême's armies swept across the
Peninsula in July, 1823, Canning sounded Rush, the
United States ambassador in London, on the possibility
of joint British and American action to prevent the
extension of Bourbon intervention across the Atlantic.
It was a momentous crisis in the history of the world :
if the Bourbons were successful, the Old World would
be made solid and safe for autocracy, the New would
be divided between antagonistic forces. If they failed,
the New World would become united for republican

independence, and the Old would be divided for future struggles between democracy and despotism.

England stood at the crossways, and the decision was not easy. George IV. was not much more enlightened than George III., nor Liverpool and Eldon than Lord North. How could those who had fought against North American independence intervene on behalf of South American insurgents ? The paternal despots had, it is true, been inconsistent in their patronage of George III.'s revolted subjects, but the age of revolution which ensued might well deter Tories from the *riposte* of encouraging other sovereigns' rebels. The political hesitation was, however, overborne by commercial interests, and a policy of principle that paid in cash had irresistible attractions. We had a vested interest in South American independence more tangible than Liberal sentiment ; and the passion for trade with Spanish colonies which had stimulated Elizabethan enterprise, Cromwellian imperialism, the Assiento and the War of Jenkins' Ear, had been gratified through the independence of the Spanish colonies. Those new markets had enabled us to bear with comparative ease the financial strain of the Napoleonic wars, and Liberal sympathy with the insurgents was subsequently fortified by the robuster fear that Ferdinand would close the door as tight as he could against British trade and bestow his preferences, if any, upon his Bourbon friends in France.

That England was out for trade rather than for political principle was a suspicion amounting to conviction in the American mind, which prevented complete co-operation between Canning and Monroe.

There was also a natural and traditional sentiment against assisting England to pay back her score against France for having abetted Lafayette ; and Adams was convinced that Canning was bent on defeating the Bourbons rather than helping republican independence. Foreign trade was less an American interest at that moment than the assertion of a political principle ; and with back doors of their own open so wide in the prairie, the United States felt less need than England to insist that their neighbours' portals should stand ajar. They had already recognised the independence of the revolted Spanish colonies, and they wanted England to do the same. But although English legionaries in their private capacity rendered yeoman service to Bolivar and his assistant liberators, the English Government was not prepared for a formal breach with its monarchical allies, and was naturally shy of republican principle.

There was a deeper distrust in Canning's mind, a distrust justified by the future. He did not like the vague but rooted idea which already underlay and was to determine the coming interpretations of the Monroe Doctrine. It was the schismatic conception of a fundamental divergence between the Old World and the New. Whatever might chance to the Old, the New World was to be an America for the Americans. North and South, the western hemisphere was to be a preserve for republican institutions, a refuge from despots and militarism, a home for peace, a vast oasis and stronghold of liberty and democracy, saved by two oceans from the infection of European exploitation and war. The New World would not intervene in the Old, the

Old must not interfere with the New; each should pursue its own course, live its own life, fashion its own ideals. Some went further than that, for there were Jingoes even in this haven of pacifist liberty; and of this New World the United States was to be the arbiter, protecting its weaker brethren against the threats of European militarism, intervening in their disputes without accepting liability for their conduct, and proclaiming its will as international law so far as relations with Europe were concerned.

There was food for anxious thought in these pretensions. The British flag flew over more American soil than the Stars and Stripes, and Pan-Americanism contained the germs of a greater menace to the British Empire than Napoleonic dreams. It seemed to shut us in on this side of the Atlantic, and to set a term to the age-long westward drift of British peoples. Further and more disconcerting than this, it appeared to abandon England to a single-handed conflict with European reaction, to leave it stewing, so to speak, in the juice of a cauldron in which it was thought to be at home, but from which it was really seeking escape. Adams thought us, but we were not, of the spirit of the Holy Alliance. Politically as well as geographically England hovered between the two worlds into which he wished to divide mankind. Cut off from the inspiration and the aspirations of the New, we might have succumbed to the Old; for outside the British Isles there was little political liberty. France was a Bourbon monarchy, Italy a collection of petty autocracies, and Metternich reigned supreme. There was hardly a British commonwealth over-seas; Australia was a convict settlement, New Zealand belonged to Maoris, South Africa had but a handful of British settlers ; while at home reform was tongue-tied by authority. The doctrine of two worlds, one released for progress, the other condemned to reaction, had nothing to recommend it to an Englishman of Canning's cast of thought. Only by maintaining the unity of the world could he maintain the bond between Great Britain and her colonies in America ; and only through the same unity could he rely upon the New World to help him in restraining the reaction of the Old. He wanted a balance where Adams would have broken the scales.

Adams' view was natural enough. American colonists were few and weak compared with the populations of European States, and he cannot be blamed for not piercing the veil of the future and foreseeing a Europe which would look to America for deliverance. If Europe could not manage her own affairs the fault was hers ; it was enough for America to make itself safe for Americans and democracy, and his ideas might seem large enough without expanding to comprehend another world. Moreover, there might be more chance of Americans being left alone if they forswore interference everywhere else ; and the burden of self-defence was sufficiently onerous. The Bourbons were not the only branch of the Holy Alliance seeking to strike root in American soil. In 1821 Russia had claimed the Pacific coast of North America almost down to Vancouver and exclusive rights of trading along it ; and the attitude of Russia was responsible for some of the feeling in America and the phrases in which it was expressed in Monroe's Presidential message in December, 1823.

That message to Congress was not in form the enunciation of a policy or a principle ; it was a statement of facts relating to public affairs, domestic as well as foreign, and of the position adopted and arguments used by the administration in the conduct of its negotiations. To a considerable extent its drafting was the work of the President's Secretary of State, John Quincy Adams, a Puritan of New England, a high-and-dry republican, and a man of narrower views but more incisive mind than the President himself. To him was apparently due the harshness and the dogmatism of some of the views expressed. But the Monroe Doctrine has been distilled from a Presidential message that dealt in a narrative way with various negotiations in language adapted to their different circumstances and never intended to be of universal application. Russian claims to monopoly along the north Pacific coast were obviously different in their character from Spanish claims to the allegiance of Spanish colonists, and still more so from Canadian claims to share in the expansion towards the west. Arguments to rebut the first were incongruous with the third, and no British Government could ever have accepted the contention that "the American continents . . . are henceforth not to be considered as subjects for future colonisation by any European Powers." Possibly by " colonisation " was meant what we should call " exploitation " ; for Adams had already expressed the view that " the whole system of modern colonisation was an abuse " and that " it was time it should come to an end," and he can hardly have meant that

Canadians had any less right to colonise Columbia than Americans California. It was left to the future to determine what the " Doctrine " meant, and this passage, which primarily referred to Russian claims, was ultimately understood to mean that existing colonies might extend into the unoccupied lands around them, but that no European Power was to obtain a fresh basis for colonial expansion on American territory.

It must, however, be remembered that the whole Presidential message was coloured by the facts that colonial autonomy was then unknown, that colonisation, therefore, meant the extension on American soil of European authority and undemocratic methods of government ; and that these in their turn were identi- fied by Americans with the principles of the Holy Alliance. It was that " system " which aroused the jealous anxiety of American statesmen, and against its extension to their continent was directed the major premiss of the President's message. It was not that he grudged the territory, but that he feared the political infection. After disclaiming any attitude save the " most friendly sentiments of anxious and interested spectators in favour of the liberty and happiness of their fellow-men " on the other side of the Atlantic, he proceeded :

" With the movements in this hemisphere we are, of necessity, more immediately connected, and by causes which must be obvious to all enlightened and impartial observers. The political system of the Allied Powers is essentially different, in this respect, from that of America. This difference proceeds from that which exists in their respective governments. And to the defence of our own, which has been achieved by so much loss of

E

blood and treasure, and matured by the wisdom of their most enlightened citizens, and under which we have enjoyed un-exampled felicity, this whole nation is devoted. We owe it there-fore to candour, and to the amicable relations existing between the United States and those Powers, to declare that we should consider any attempt on their part to extend their dominion to any portion of this hemisphere as dangerous to our peace and safety. With the existing colonies or dependencies of any Euro-pean Power we have not interfered, and shall not interfere. But with the governments who have declared their independence and maintained it, and whose independence we have, on great consideration, and on just principles, acknowledged, we could not view any interposition for the purpose of oppressing them, or controlling, in any other manner, their destiny, by any Euro-pean Power, in any other light than as the manifestation of an unfriendly disposition towards the United States."

The counterpart of this policy of throwing the pro-tection of the United States over democracy and re-publicanism in both American continents consisted in the repudiation of all ideas of interfering with auto-cracy elsewhere. It was the western hemisphere and not the world that was to be made safe for democracy.

" Our policy in regard to Europe," continued the President, " which was adopted at an early stage of the wars which have so long agitated that quarter of the globe, nevertheless remains the same, which is not to interfere in the internal concerns of any of its Powers, to consider the government *de facto* as the legitimate government for us ; to cultivate friendly relations with it, and to preserve those relations by a frank, firm and manly policy, meet-ing in all instances the just claims of every Power, submitting to injuries from none. But, in regard to these continents, circum-stances are eminently and conspicuously different. It is impos-sible that the Allied Powers should extend their political system to any portion of either continent without endangering our peace and happiness ; nor can any one believe that our southern brethren, if left to themselves, would adopt it of their own accord. It is equally impossible, therefore, that we should behold such interposition, in any form, with indifference. . . . It is still the true policy of the United States to leave the parties to themselves, in the hope that other Powers will pursue the same course."

The passage about colonisation, provoked by Russian claims on the Pacific coast, and the wider implications in the President's message were overshadowed by the immediate effect of his pronouncement upon the South American problem. Whatever might be the difference in point of view between the British and American Governments, and, however inconvenient the Monroe Doctrine might prove to be for the future relations between the two Powers, it was felt on both sides of the Atlantic that on the immediate issue they stood together, and their attitude was decisive. The project of a European Congress to discuss intervention in South America was dropped, and the most reactionary governments sought to follow the British example by developing trade in the newly-opened and independent markets. Ferdinand alone renewed his ineffective protests. But there was secret dismay in the councils of the Holy Alliance ; the message gave great offence in Prussia, and Metternich repeated his prophecies of the calamities which the New World would bring upon the Old. Opinion was not by any means unanimous in Great Britain, and Canning repudiated the right of any nation to veto colonisation on the American continents. The future alone could settle the problems involved in that claim, and Canning could not foresee how the grant of self-government to our colonies was to reconcile their growth with American repugnance to the extension of the " political system " of the Holy Alliance. Apart from its effect upon the domestic fortunes of the British Empire, that Liberal policy was an essential ingredient in Anglo-American friendship ; and the reaction of the Monroe Doctrine upon the cause of progress in Europe is an important but unexplored aspect of nineteenth-century history. Assuredly the co-operation of Great Britain and the United States in the liberation of South America weakened the Holy Alliance in Europe ; and making the New World safe for democracy made the Old World less secure in its Legitimism.

The Presidential message achieved its immediate object, and, content with this practical success, the people of the United States allowed their interest in the " Doctrine " to slumber until later crises sent them searching for a principle on which to base their later views. The Doctrine had *ex hypothesi* no application to the relations of purely American States with one another, and disputes between the United States and the now independent Mexico over their frontiers were settled, uniformly to the advantage of the United States, by war or by diplomacy without reference to the President's message. But whenever the dispute was between an American republic and a European Power possessing territory in the western hemisphere, there was a tendency to revert to, and improve upon, the passage in which Monroe had seemed to veto colonisation, and against which Canning had protested. The Doctrine came to the front again in the disputes over the Oregon territory and the delimitation of the frontiers of Maine. But the most resounding application of the Doctrine was the veto imposed by the United States upon Napoleon III.'s adventure in Mexico. Feeling the need of an imperialistic foreign policy, and finding an opportunity during the American Civil War, the French Emperor abetted the candidature of the unfortunate Maximilian for an imperial throne in Mexico, and despatched a French expedition to support him against his rebellious subjects. This was clearly a case of extending the " political system " of Europe to American soil, and the moment the Civil War was liquidated, the United States stepped in with a re-assertion of Monroe's Doctrine. Once more the European Power had no choice but to submit.

Here there was no extension or even straining of Monroe's message, but the same cannot be said of some later appeals to the " Doctrine." It was even at times expanded to mean a United States protectorate over the whole hemisphere, and in this way it came to be something of a bugbear to Latin American States. They were glad enough to avail themselves of the protection it afforded against intervention by great European Powers, but they naturally feared its implied menace to their own independence of the United States, and there have been moments at which South American politicians have dreamed and talked of a United States of South America, less as a safeguard against European colonisation or autocracy than as a measure of defence against the pretensions of the United States of the North. For such fears there was some justification from a wider point of view than the South American ; for " spread-eagleism " is much the same in its fundamentals as Old World imperialism, and no country, not even the United States, is quite immune from the spirit we now identify with Prussia. The creation of the Panama Canal afforded a natural outlet for such sentiments. " I guess," remarked an American in 1913, " that the United States can do what it likes with its own property." " But what," he was asked, " about the Clayton-Bulwer Treaty ? " " Damn the Treaty," was the laconic reply, upon which no Prussian talking of Belgian scraps of paper could have improved.

There were, indeed, occasions upon which American orators claimed in effect that, so far as American affairs were concerned, the will of the United States was *ipso facto* international law, or rather that the whole American hemisphere was a unit, subject to the suzerainty of the United States and therefore immune, so far as its other States were concerned, from the ordinary liabilities and responsibilities to international law. A South American republic, for instance, was not to be made accountable to a European Power for its debts or its conduct towards the subjects of that Power unless the claim seemed reasonable to the United States. When in 1895-6 an acute boundary dispute arose between Great Britain and Venezuela, the United States intervened and grounded its intervention upon the Monroe Doctrine. There was nothing in President Monroe's message to justify such an interpretation : Monroe had declared it to be the true policy of the United States in 1823 to leave the parties to themselves, and no one suspected Great Britain in 1895 of harbouring any design to annex or colonise Venezuela. Still less, as Lord Salisbury pointed out, was there any ground in international law for an intervention of this nature by a third party in the relations between two sovereign States. Unless the United States would—and it would not—make itself responsible for the conduct of disorderly Latin American republics, it could not object to European Powers holding those republics responsible for themselves.

Law and logic were both on the side of Great Britain ; but there was something greater than either on the side of the United States, though it did not justify the case as it was stated by Secretary Olney. The Americans had a pronounced and natural fear of militarism in all its forms, and the more it dominated Europe the more they were determined to resist its introduction into America. But force was still regarded as the ultimate arbiter in all disputes, and unarmed American republics would have to yield, whatever the merits of their case, in their disputes with well-equipped European Powers. Hence, sooner or later they, too, would be compelled to arm unless some other method were found and enforced for the settlement of disputes. The United States had no standing by international law in the disputes between European Powers and American republics, but it had a legitimate and overwhelming interest in the settlement of those disputes by other means than war. If they were not, one American State after another would arm, and the New World would become as militarist as the Old. The United States did not intend any interference in these disputes beyond insisting that they should be settled by arbitration and not by force of arms ; thus the temptation to militarism in the American continents would be averted, and the New World would avoid that danger to democracy which threatened it in the Old. There may have been no justification by the letter of international law for even this claim ; but international law had not shown itself in militarist Europe to be worth the sacrifice to it in America of the principle of arbitration on which the United States had taken its stand ; and before 1914 Europe had practically admitted that its disputes in the New World would have to be settled by new methods.

The New World had thus been made not only safe for democracy but safe for peace ; and had the assumption, on which the Monroe Doctrine rested, of a complete separation between the New World and the Old been valid, that doctrine would have achieved complete success within the sphere it had marked out. But there is no limited liability in humanity's affairs, and the Monroe Doctrine failed to divide the world into two. The annihilation of space by steam and electricity broke down the natural and the artificial isolation of mankind. The two worlds became one, and neither could repose in its peace and in its democracy indifferent to the other. The United States had grown too big, and the world had grown too small, to admit of the existence of two antagonistic systems of international conduct. It was impossible to have one hemisphere dominated by militarism and another trusting in peace, to settle eastern disputes by the argument of force and western disputes by the force of argument. For the nation accustomed to war regarded it as the final arbitrament wherever the conflict might arise, and the people which believed in arbitration also believed in its universal application. One or the other must become the general rule common to both the worlds; and inasmuch as no arbitration could compel the believer in war to abandon his weapons, the apostles of peace were driven to drawing the sword to disarm him.

This war is, therefore, a civil war because the world has become a single community. That sounds like a paradox in the midst of a world-wide strife; but civil wars have often been the unconscious symptoms and the growing-pains of unity. They are disputes over the articles of association, and they only arise when the association has been formed or is in process of formation. No civil war was ever fought between parties who had agreed to separate; and if the New World had found it possible to live without the Old, the United States would not have intervened. So, too, our Wars of the Roses were fought because England had become a nation and there was no room within it for both a Lancastrian and a Yorkist State; the significance of those two parties was not that they divided England, but that they united so many local factions into two national parties which struggled for control of the national State. Thus, too, the Wars of Religion in France changed Breton and Gascon, Norman and Provençal, from provincials into two national parties, and the triumph of one of them made France a nation. In the same way the American Civil War was a symptom of growing unity; it showed that the States were becoming too much united to speak with a double voice on such questions as slavery and the Constitution, and the present war has shown that the whole world is too much one to have two halves governed by mutually destructive principles.

We cannot escape our common fate by isolation, and the Monroe Doctrine has crossed the Atlantic, shedding its American limitations, to make the whole world safe for freedom. That was the cause that had brought other scions of our race across other seas earlier in the war ; but there is a profound significance in the moving sight of this reunion of the Anglo-Saxon world. Liberty is the common bond ; to some we gave it freely, others won it in our despite. But liberty has healed the breach which the refusal of it made ; and the children of those old Pilgrim Fathers who went forth with tears bearing their precious seed, have come again rejoicing, bringing their sheaves with them, sheaves in the shape of Metternich's " calamities " of judgment and retribution for the architects of ruin and the autocrats of war. And amid all the desolation of the conflict, the defection of false or feeble friends, and the deferment of hope, we yet may use of Freedom and her children the words which Shakespeare used of old-time England and her princes :

> " Now these her children are come home again,
> Come the three corners of the world in arms,
> And we shall shock them. Nought shall make us rue
> If Freedom to herself do rest but true."

CHAPTER V

THE DEVELOPMENT OF AFRICA

By SIR H. H. JOHNSTON, G.C.M.G., K.C.B.

FROM some scanty evidence collected from caverns and
grottoes in Mediterranean lands, from the earliest
records of Egyptian art, from the rock-engravings of
North Africa and the Sahara, from similar discoveries
in southernmost Africa, we are entitled to surmise that
the white man of Europe, since a period so remote that
perhaps he was, at the beginning of it, only as light-
skinned as the Ainu of Japan, has interfered with
Africa, has sought in some fashion to turn its natural
resources to account. *Homo sapiens* as a species may
well have arisen in South-west Asia, and the tradition of
the Garden of Eden be one of those unaccountable race-
memories. During the long-drawn-out Ice Ages and in
their recurrent periods of warm climate, the original
human species from which all existing human races are
derived, specialised into three main sub-species or
varieties : the White Man, the Mongol and the Negro.
The Australoid, still living in Australia, represents
more nearly than any other living race the semblance
of *Homo sapiens* in his basic type as he wandered
through Europe, Asia, Africa, the Malay Archipelago
and perhaps even America many, many thousands of
years ago ; and there is a little evidence in North and
East Africa to indicate that the first humans who
colonised the least forested portions of Africa were

rather more of the Australoid than of the highly specialised Negro type.

But climatic and other factors during the Pleistocene gradually moulded this primitive ancestor of modern Man into White Man or European, Mongol or North Asiatic and Amerindian, and Negro ; besides leaving over a great number of intermediate types that belonged less definitely to these extreme forms. The White Man and the Mongol grappled with glacial conditions of life ; the ancestors of the Negro turned to the warm belt of the Old World ; colonised the Mediterranean Basin, Africa, Southern Persia, India, Malaysia and many of the Pacific archipelagoes ; in a very primitive and less differentiated form they even reached Eastern Australia and finally Tasmania.

In Africa, from Algeria to the Cape of Good Hope, the ancestral Negro found himself in a region better provided on the whole with a varied and unfailing food supply than Europe, North or Central Asia ; and far more extensive and continuous than Southern India and Malaysia. The sterility of the Sahara was not then observable. There were broad, ever-flowing rivers, there were shallow lakes and swamps where there are now dry watercourses (some of them full of the bones of hippopotami), salt-encrusted depressions or shifting sands. The better-watered regions of the Sahara produced wild dates and figs, tamarinds and " monkey-bread " ; and nearly all the area of this now forbidding desert teemed with game, and its lakes and rivers with fish. North Africa was a hunter's paradise ; so were East Africa, South Africa, the Valley of the Nile and the plateaux of Nigeria. The dense forests no doubt were

shunned, partly because of the fierce gorillas and chim-
panzis, the leopards and snakes they sheltered; but
there was no danger of starvation in their depths. You
could live on succulent fungi, on wild honey, on fat
white beetle-grubs, on wild fruits and nuts of many
kinds, on the larvæ of ants and the adult termites, on
gums, on the hearts of palm-trees, on birds, nestlings
and eggs. In short, the aboriginal Negro when he
spread out over Tropical Africa from North Africa and
the Nile Valley and Delta found life so comparatively
easy in winterless Africa that he let his intellect lie
fallow; the while the White and Yellow sub-species
of Man were sharpening their wits, strengthening their
wills and their powers of endurance by fighting the
glacial climates and the long winters of the northern
temperate zone.

Forty or fifty thousand years ago there were still
existing Negroes and Negroids of a rather Asiatic type in
Southern Europe; and though the western Mediterranean may have again pierced the Straits of Gibraltar,
Italy, Sicily, Malta and Tunis were still united by a
gradually dissolving land-bridge. The White men of
Central, Western and Eastern Europe pushed the
Negroes before them through Italy and through Syria
into North Africa and Egypt; then in course of time
followed them. The Negro type passed up the valley
of the Nile into the Sudan and East Africa; across the
Sahara by the upland bridge of Tibesti, into the Chad
basin; along the Atlantic coast into Senegal and the
Niger valley; and again from Nubia and Sennar into
Darfur and Kordofan. The Pygmies permeated the
dense forests of the West and Centre, and in course of

time were succeeded and supplanted by the taller
Forest Negroes. A special type of desert Negro, the
Bushman, passed down through Eastern Africa into
South Africa.

Concurrently with these human migrations there
were taking place, rather rapidly, climatic changes
north and south of the Tropics which restricted rainfall, so that great sandy wastes and dry steppes made
the Sahara more and more uninhabitable for man and
beast, while much of South-west Africa was similarly
afflicted. This change had a potent effect on the opening
up of Africa. Between twenty thousand and two
thousand years ago it made the Sahara an obstacle of
increasing potency in the southward paths of the White
Man's migrations and more and more isolated the
Negro. The Nile valley, however, remained as a north-
and-south route into and out of Tropical Africa.

We seem to discern trickles of White-Man-migration
into southernmost Africa, possibly by the East Coast
route, at a period which may be guessed at as far back in
time as thirty to twenty thousand years ago. When I
use the term " White Man " I do so in a very generalised
sense : I mean some such type as the Crô-Magnon of
Europe, Asia and North Africa, appearing in South
Africa as the " Strandlooper " ; in appearance not
unlike the Sikh or Panjabi of India, of tall or very tall
stature, great brain capacity, rather rugged, high-cheek-
boned face-outline, possibly yellow- or brown-skinned,
but an intellectual as well as a physical giant. The Crô-
Magnon type in Europe and North Africa is associated
with those wonderful pictures, engravings and sculp-
tures of the animals he hunted and ate ; and similarly

the Strandlooper of South Africa is thought to be the originator and inspirer of Bushman art.

Egypt some twelve thousand years ago—all this chronology is intended more symbolically than statistically—was strongly invaded by some more definitely " White Man " race from Syria and Northern Arabia, which found the Delta of the Nile inhabited by a race of Pygmy Negroids very like in appearance to the Negro Pygmies of New Guinea, and not very dissimilar from the Congo Forest Pygmies of the present day. Them they chased out of existence. These first " White " invaders of Egypt were the ancestors of the Hamitic peoples, the Libyans, Galla, Somali, Ethiopians. We are entitled to conjecture that they next swept westward over Tripoli, Tunis, Algeria and Morocco, much as the Arabs did in historical times. They probably found North Africa then still retaining vestiges of its former Negro—and even of the much earlier Australoid—population, but mainly inhabited by a light- or white-skinned, black-haired and very hairy race which might be termed Iberian, not without kinship with the Basque and the Alpine, Dinaric and Caucasic peoples of Europe. On this Iberian or Berber race, then the leading human type of Western Europe, they imposed the Hamitic speech. Counter-invasions of North-east Africa, from Egypt to Abyssinia, took place which brought this Iberian type, these Lybian or Berber people, eastward. The Hamites and the Lybians in the Neolithic Age succeeded the Crô-Magnons as tentative penetrators and developers of Tropical Africa. They had domesticated the ox, or more probably had received the domestic breeds of cattle from Egypt,

which in turn had them from Syria. Horses they may
have obtained likewise from Egypt, if not from Spain ;
asses from Nubia or the Sahara. With the aid of riding
or transport (pack) animals they may have passed from
oasis to oasis across a Sahara then much less formidable
as a sand waste. Probably also they found it possible
to travel along the Atlantic coast. Another and much
more effective route by which the early Hamite influenced the Western Sudan was from Egypt to Darfur
and Kordofan and thus into the Chad basin ; or up
the Nile valley into Uganda ; from Somaliland likewise
into Equatorial East Africa and the Zangian coast.

In prehistoric Arabia a great struggle had been taking
place between intelligent Man of early Neolithic times
and recalcitrant Nature. There is not much trace of
any ancient Negro population of Arabia, except where
it merges into the Mesopotamian lands of the Persian
Gulf. Perhaps, what with volcanic eruptions and what
with a marked acceleration of desiccation in Central
and West Central Arabia, the early Negro and Negroid
peoples of that peninsula may have died out and have
left the habitable lands of the west, south and south-
east open to early White Man colonisation from Syria
and Mesopotamia. About seven or eight thousand
years ago we may surmise that these Proto-Semitic and
Hamitic peoples of Arabia were hard put to it to subsist
on the scanty and irregular supply of rain. They
became, therefore, increasingly industrious in stone
work, in first rough and then fine masonry, which
might dam up mountain torrents and make large
cisterns to supply drinking water for themselves and
their herds and to irrigate those fields where they, in

the dawn of Neolithic civilisation, were planting their cereals and root crops. Some of these tribes, however—of expert stone-masons and quarriers—grew impatient with this losing fight against Nature and gazed across the narrower parts of the Red Sea at the blue silhouettes of the Abyssinian mountains. Doubtless also they had canoes and even the beginnings of ships on the Red Sea, and in these they crossed in small and large parties over to the Suakin and Abyssinian coast. Thence they made their way overland into the Nile Valley and so on down the Nile till they became the Dynastic Race of Upper and Lower Egypt, applying to the lands of the Lower Nile that amazing mastery over stone which they had acquired in Arabia.

They brought with them to this part of North-east Africa a language and a racial type which were compounded of Semitic and Hamitic elements, with perhaps some other monosyllabic strain, derived—like some of their physical characteristics—from a Mongolian blend of Babylonian origin. They were, however, sufficiently akin to the Hamitic populations of the Red Sea Littoral (the "Fuzzie-wuzzies" of to-day) and the Libyo-Hamites of Lower Egypt to fuse with these antecedent peoples and create the Egyptian type and nation which has played such a glorious part in the history of Man and of Africa.

From about five thousand years ago Egypt began half unconsciously the development of Negro Africa. There was some slight degree of race permeation which carried Egyptian facial features of the Pharaonic type right into Equatorial Africa and into the basin of the Niger, and Egyptian fashions in hairdressing and

F

clothing into the Congo basin. Egyptian types of musical instruments penetrated to North Congoland and to the Niger ; Egyptian notions of architecture—stone imitated by clay—penetrated to westernmost Nigeria. Egyptian games spread all over Africa except the dense forests of the Pygmies and the Forest Negroes. Most important of all these influences, Egyptian cultivated plants and domesticated animals travelled from tribe to tribe till they had reached all parts of Africa save a few portions of the densest forests or the haunts of the wild Bushmen in South African rocks and deserts.

It is remarkable in our study of the development of Africa to realise that down to the nineteenth century nearly all the utilisation of Africa's natural resources has proceeded from foreign influence : I mean, non-Negro inspiration. I do not myself believe the Negro invented any art. Up to the present he has only been a copyist. Some writers on metallurgy have sought to show that the Negro—in Africa, at any rate—originated the forging and use of iron. I do not hold this view, though I cannot give my reasons here. Negro Africa, like North Africa (not Egypt), was very rich in iron ore. I think the use of iron arose—independently perhaps—among the Iberians of North Africa, either by the communication of the idea from Spain or from Syria (through the early Phœnicians) or from the Aryan invaders of Sicily and Greece. From Mauritania—North Africa—the smelting and use of iron spread into Egypt and also across the Sahara into the Sudan, and thence was carried over a great deal of West and Central Africa by the Bantu and Semi-Bantu tribes who originated in Nigeria.

But the Negro never produced a cultivated plant from

an African wild species ; nor a domestic animal or bird from out of the rich African fauna. What were his domestic animals and plants when Africa was discovered by the Portuguese ? Just about what he had derived from Asia through Egypt and Abyssinia : the Durra grain (*Holcus*), millet, eleusine, rice, sugar cane, hemp, sesamum, pumpkins, gourds, the banana and plantain, and, on the Indian Ocean coast, the coco-nut palm ; the dog (from remote Palæolithic times), the goat, sheep, domestic fowl and (in the Muhammadan belt) the pigeon. The horse had been introduced into the Sudan, but nowhere south of the Equator, and the ass was used as a pack animal also in the Sudan and Somaliland and the Zangian coast. None of these cultivated plants had an African origin, nor any of the domesticated animals except the ass ; and as a beast under control, subdued to man's requirements, the domestic ass was an Egyptian or Hamite invention, not a Negro experiment.

Yet in Negro Africa there are wild grains which by cultivation might become edible and digestible ; there are wild Musaceæ akin to the Asiatic ancestor of the banana and plantain, there are countless roots, nuts, fruits, tubers, gums, sugary saps, oily seeds, palatable salads, spinaches, green vegetables to be derived from wild trees, plants, reeds and grasses which might have their food-value centupled by cultivation and selection. About the only wild African products to which the Negro has turned his attention as an agriculturist are the ground-nut (*Arachis*), the yam (*Dioscorea*), the *Colocasia* aroid (with large tubers like the Taro yam of the Pacific archipelagoes), and the oil palm. The original parent form of the pea-nut or ground nut (*Arachis hypogæa*) may have originated in West Africa, though some botanists claim Tropical America as its home. The various cultivated yams of West and Central Africa can be traced back to an African progenitor ; the oil palm is indigenous to Africa. As to the origin of the *Colocasia* aroid (the " Coco yam " of West Africa) even that may have come from Tropical Asia and have owed its introduction to the same human agency as the cultivated plantain. It is thought to have been known to the ancient Egyptians under the name of Kulkaz (which gives rise to the Latin name, *Colocasia*). With regard to *Elais guineensis*, the oil palm—which I predict is going to become a matter of world concern, so valuable is it as a source of food, soap, lubricants, alcohol, sugar and fibre—it has nowhere been found in West and West Central Africa in a purely wild state, that is to say away from man's knowledge and control. The really wild *Elais guineensis* is still to be met with in the island of Zanzibar, in North-west Nyasaland, the eastern basin of Tanganyika and the southern part of Congoland. But in these regions its properties are either unknown to the natives or are not worth over-much attention on their part, as the supply of oil is poor in amount and quality. It may therefore be that in the taller, more specialised oil palms of the Congo basin and the West African coast-lands we have a native product that has been developed to some extent by the Negro. Yet here again we must trace " white " influence in the nineteenth century. It is not quite a hundred years since the value of palm oil was first realised in Europe. Its great vogue began with the making of railways, because it was such a useful lubricant. Since the palm-oil trade started on the West African coast there is no doubt that the Negro has given much attention to the cultivation and improvement of this invaluable tree.

Africa teems with metallic wealth and with all manner of precious stones. Yet, but for " White Man " influence, early and late, these riches would lie there in the rocks and river-beds unregarded. I have already expressed my belief that iron-working was a White Man's notion originally and not a Negro's ; similarly " White " influence from Egypt or North Africa and from Arabia seems to have prompted the smelting and forging of copper and the supplanting of stone by copper implements, concurrently with those of iron. Iron and copper ores were simply called " stones " in the earlier types of African languages, and were used as extra hard stones before, through foreign teaching, the natives learnt the processes of smelting, casting and forging. Before the White or semi-White Man from Egypt or Mauritania pointed out the value and charm of Gold, the Negro let nuggets and gold-dust lie where water action revealed them. Over all Bantu Africa, from the Northern Congo and Cameroons and the Great Lakes to Cape Colony and Zululand, there is no indigenous root-word for " gold," nor are there widespread and archaic roots for copper (as there are for iron). Either gold is not differentiated at all in the Bantu mind as a substance of any interest, or it is designated by a word which can be traced back to the Arabic ; as though the Eastern Bantu Negro had first had gold pointed out to him by some adventurous Arab in Islamic or pre-Islamic times. I very strongly suspect that the gold of the Ashanti and Senegambian river-beds was first noticed by bold Negroid merchants and prospectors ranging westwards from the Chad basin, whither an indirect " White Man " influence must have penetrated in the last thousand years before the Christian era, proceeding from the Hellenised Egypt, the Phœnician and Roman North Africa. But the great appreciation of gold on the Gold Coast and in Bambarra, as also in the regions south of the Lower Zambezi, only began as recently as the Islamic period, let us say from after the Arabising of Negro Africa on a great scale which set in in the eleventh century A.D. Although Africa teems with precious stones—garnets nearly all over it ; diamonds in South, South-west and South-central Africa and in Liberia ; emeralds in the North-east ; many different forms of corundum and of rock crystal—the primitive Negro never sought for his ornaments in his own land by shallow excavation ; he preferred to deck himself during the past two thousand five hundred years with glass and porcelain beads manufactured in Egypt and Italy and percolating through his savagery by devious channels of hand-to-hand trade. When ancient graves are opened on the Gold Coast or excavated ground is sifted in Kavirondo or Liberia, we find therein this evidence of an overland trade between Equatorial Africa and the Mediterranean lands which must have reached back four, six, ten centuries beyond the epoch-making invasion of Islam.

This series of race movements which commenced with the conquest of Egypt by the Arabs in the seventh century A.D., assumed special prominence in the tenth and eleventh centuries, and by degrees forced intelligent and awakened Europe to occupy itself with Africa. But in order to embrace the entire history of the Development of Africa in this rapid survey, I should fill up the gap I have left after alluding to the spread of Egyptian influence ; which, so far as Negro Africa was concerned, reached its maximum effect about a thousand years before Christ. The Phœnicians at the close of the previous millennium had established themselves on the Syrian coast and on the Red Sea. They must have begun to explore the East African coast beyond the Straits of Bab-al-Mandib, and it is quite possible one of their bold sea captains accepted the commission of the Pharaoh Niku to circumnavigate the African continent. More than a thousand years before the Christian era, they had established trading stations on the north coast of Africa, and after the sixth century B.C. Carthage, the daughter of Tyre, took up the early Semiticising of Mauritania and carried it much farther. Carthaginian ships sailed round the Atlantic coast in about the sixth century B.C., and (according to a much battered account transmitted from Punic to Greek and Greek to Latin) reached to what we should now call the eastern extremity of Sierra Leone.

Greeks colonised Cyrene, between Egypt and Tripoli, in the sixth and seventh centuries B.C., and probably settled to a considerable degree in Tunis from the Greek colonies in Sicily. Greek influence on Negro arts has been traced right across the Sahara to Nigeria and North Cameroon, not altogether fancifully.

Persia conquered Egypt under Cambyses, five hundred years before the Christian era ; and after that dividing-point in time, when Rome weakened, Persian influence —with India behind Persia—began to affect the development of Africa. The earliest invasion of the Persians, which finished Egyptian independence from 525 B.C. till the present day, brought with it the domestic fowl. Though the Negro had never thought of domesticating the guinea-fowl or the francolin, he appreciated enormously this gift of *Gallus bankiva* from Asia, and in something like two thousand years Chanticlere and Dame Partlet had spread all over Negro and Negroid Africa, excepting only among the nomad Bushmen and Hottentots in the south and the Pygmies in the densest forests of the centre.

The most effective amount of Persian influence on African culture, however, was introduced through Arabia into Abyssinia in the fifth and sixth centuries of the Christian era ; and through the Shirazi settlements on the Northern Zangian Coast in the eleventh and twelfth centuries.

Greek influence, which began prehistorically as far back as the times of Troy, was of course greatly enhanced by the conquests of Alexander, resulting in a Hellenised Egypt. Greek influence under the Ptolemies reached Abyssinia, the middle Nile, and the island of Sokotra. It was scarcely arrested by the Roman supersession of this Greek dynasty, and was strongly revived in North-east Africa and in Tunis and Tripoli under the Byzantine Empire.

Mention must also be made of the Jewish rôle among the developers of Africa, both before and after the Fall of Jerusalem. Alexander's conquests and the Greek kingdom in Syria paved the way for Jewish emigration to Alexandria and Carthage. From much earlier times there seems to have sprung up a sea trade between

Judæa and the Abyssinian coast ports, by the intermediary of the Sabæan State in Western Arabia. After the Roman destruction of Jewish independence and the dispersal of the Jews, thousands and thousands of them emigrated to North Africa—Cyrene, Tripoli, Carthage above all, and Morocco. Smaller numbers spread themselves over Western Arabia and reinforced the Jewish settlements in Abyssinia. In North Africa the Jews, speaking Aramaic and remembering Hebrew, must have found it easy to step into the shoes of the Phœnician Carthaginians, whose language (so closely allied to Hebrew and Aramaic) still lingered in Southern Tunisia as a spoken tongue. The warlike Berbers, who had never really liked the Romans and consequently were not well inclined to Christianity, took up the Jew warmly, and many became proselytes to the Jewish faith. There is a tradition in North Africa that enterprising Jews criss-crossed the northern Sahara desert (with the aid of the camel and the ass) and reached certain of the oases which were found uninhabited or only inhabited by Negroes—the Neolithic hunter-folk having died out. There really seems to be some ground for the theory of Richard Lander, the Niger explorer, that Jewish traders penetrated to Borgu in Central Nigeria in the fifth or sixth century of this era, and there implanted remarkable religious beliefs, an amalgam of Christianity and Judaism which lingered in Borgu down to the nineteenth century and is perhaps not yet quite extinct.

Greeks and Romans between the fifth century B.C. and the sixth century A.D. had gleaned and transmitted to writing and to charts much information as to the geography of Africa ; as to the outline of its coasts from the Senegal River on the west to Zanzibar on the east. They had acquired a general idea of the course and origin of the Nile and the Mountains of the Full Moon (Ruwenzori) and the Nile lakes ; the existence of Kilimanjaro ; of Lake Chad ; of the Niger ; of the Atlas Mountains. But it was the sweeping of the Islamic Arabs over Africa which of all recorded race movements most completely tore aside the veil in which Ethiopia had hidden herself from her White brother. The Græco-Roman civilisation had done little more than sketch the general outline of the African continent between its westernmost and easternmost extremities. The Arab and the Arabised Berber, Syrian and Persian traversed the Sudan from sea to sea, and revealed its Negro states, its lakes and rivers and mountain chains to an almost incredulous Europe. Pre-Islamic Arabs had undoubtedly colonised patches of the East African coast as far south as Inyambane, as well as northern Madagascar. But this entry of the civilised, clothed Semite into South-east Africa (so superior in culture and intelligence to the naked, primitive Bantu Negroes that they termed him " God " or " Demi-god "), greatly influenced the history and development of Zangia, between Somaliland and Sofala. It brought into the stream of African commerce the Chinese under their Tartar Emperors ; it drew the Indian, the Baluch, the Persian into Africa. It negrified the Malayo-Polynesian inhabitants of Madagascar by introducing amongst them hundreds of thousands of Bantu Negroes brought over as slaves in a very easy servitude.

The knowledge of Africa thus acquired began to reach Europe through those Crusades which really commenced in the ninth and tenth centuries by the recoil of the Romano-Gothic and Franco-Roman Christians of Spain and Provence against the Arab-Berber conquerors of Spain and Portugal. In spite of the hatred between these warring Christians and Muhammadans, they communicated much knowledge to one another, and in the Epic of Roland, composed by an Anglo-Norman clerk in the eleventh century, you can pick up much information as to the peoples of North Africa, the Sahara and the Northern Sudan, communicated of course through Spain. The great Crusades to recover the Holy Land from the Turk commenced in the eleventh century. They drew Englishmen, Irishmen, French, Italians, Germans, Flemings and Portuguese into Africa. When the Holy Land was lost, the effort nevertheless drove the Arab-Berber from Portugal, and the impetus carried the Portuguese into Morocco.

From Morocco the Portuguese were drawn into continuing the plucky attempts of Genoese and Mallorcan sea-captains to explore the Atlantic coasts of Africa. In a hundred years, the Portuguese, not without help from the Venetians and the Jews, had revealed the outline and limits of the African continent, had placed Madagascar on the map, and entered the Red Sea from the south. In the development not only of Africa but of the whole world, Old and New, Portugal has crowned herself with everlasting glory by the bold achievements and the calculated science in navigation of her fifteenth and sixteenth century explorers. The opening up of

Africa by the Portuguese between 1446 and the close of the nineteenth century has conferred on Africa an ineffaceable impression and many lasting benefits. The West African and a few of the East African languages teem with borrowed Portuguese words to express ideas and objects new to the Black Man in the earlier centuries. Portugal, almost entirely and mainly, introduced into Africa from Tropical America, India and Malaysia the tobacco plant (which replaced the poisonous narcotic, hemp), the invaluable maize cereal, the coco-nut palm (in West Africa), the sugar cane, the orange and lime, manioc (arrowroot, tapioca), the sweet potato, tomato, onion, pineapple, papaw, melon and the cultivated cotton plant ; the domestic pig, the Casarca duck, the turkey.

A survey of the historical course of the Development of Africa cannot leave out of account certain great movements from within, even if in these cases there is very little written history to guide us ; chiefly native traditions and the deductions to be formed from language-study and archæology. Besides the great effect which was produced on the Development of Africa and its resources by the invasion of the continent or the conquests on the continent and its coast by non-Negro peoples from Asia and Europe (or the influence radiating from their seed-plots in North Africa, Egypt and Abyssinia) vast changes and on the whole some progress towards civilisation arose from native movements, provoked nearly always by some form of White Man interference, stimulation, or racial mixture. There were at least eight of these tidal waves of conquering tribes of the first order of importance, and other less extensive shiftings of populations which should be given consideration in a rightly-written History of Africa. The eight would consist of : (1) The ferment in Northern Nigeria which created the Hausa language and the Hausa nation (this was probably due to the establishment two to three thousand years ago of Hamitic trade depots in the North Central Sudan) ; (2) the Mandingo or Melle Empire in West Africa ; (3) the Soñghai Empire ; (4) the tremendous surge and expansion of the Bantu and Semi-Bantu peoples, which, radiating from a centre in Eastern Nigeria, carried the Semi-Bantu languages as far west as the Gambia river, and the closely-allied Bantu tongues over the whole of Central and Southern Africa, save only a small portion in the south-west (Cape Colony and Namakwaland) ; (5) the analogous expansion over West and West Central Africa of the Fula [1] race ; (6) the migration south-eastward of the Nilotic negroes, which carried tribes of them to the Victoria Nyanza and Lake Rudoph, and their specialised branch, the Masai, far into Equatorial East Africa within sight of the Indian Ocean ; (7) and (8) the Nyam-nyam and Mañgbettu domination, nearly side by side, in the southern Bahr-al-Ghazal and on the Upper Wele.

Among the subsidiary race or tribal movements which affected in a lesser way the destiny of Africa I would enumerate the (9) migration of the Hottentots from some part of Equatorial East Africa south of the Victoria

---

[1] Possibly a Negroid hybrid with the Neolithic White Men of North Africa, originating in Mauritania and passing down the Atlantic coast to find a first area of expansion in Senegambia and the valley of the Upper Niger.

Nyanza to South-west Africa (via Tanganyika) ; (10) the rise to power of the Fung-Arab hybrids in the Egyptian Sudan, which stimulated the creation of powerful Negroid states in Darfur and Wadai ; (11) the creation of the Bornu kingdom in the western basin of Lake Chad by Kanuri-Kanem Negroids coming from the Tibu country of the Central Sahara ; (12) the rise of the Juku power on the central Benue ; (13) of the Yorubas in Southern Nigeria ; (14) the Ehwe in Dahomé ; (15) the Mosi in the Upper Volta basin ; and (16) the Agni peoples of the Gold Coast, Ashanti and Ivory coast.

The great Bantu movement (No. 4 in my list), which did much to open up Africa to superior races of higher culture than that of the Pygmy and the Forest Negro, should in its history be further subdivided into the development of the Bushoñgo culture and the Luba-Lunda Kingdoms of South-central Congoland; the ancient Buganda empire of the Victoria Nyanza with the allied Nyoro dynasties; the Monomotapa (Mwene-mutapa) kingdom in South-east Africa ; the invasion of Eastern Africa (Zambezia) by the " Jagas " or Bajok ; the Fang migrations in western Equatorial Africa ; and the northward return marches of the Zulu-Kaffir tribes and the Bechuana-Basuto people. The last-mentioned series of warlike migrations took place during the first three quarters of the nineteenth century under the observation of White pioneers in exploration and mission work. It affected Eastern Africa as far north as the vicinity of Lakes Nyasa, Tanganyika and the western Victoria Nyanza.

Unfortunately, both Spaniards and Portuguese

(followed with no great interval of time by the Dutch,
French and English) looked upon the Africa of the
sixteenth, seventeenth, eighteenth and early nineteenth
centuries as little more than a slave market for the
supply of labour to the New World. The slave trade
had evidently been the curse of Africa from the tenth
century of the Christian era. In Egyptian times, in the
Greek and Latin domination of Egypt and North
Africa, Negro slaves were obtained from the Saharan
oases and from the Nile regions ; partly as tribute and
partly by their voluntary migration to the Lands of
Light. Slave-raiding for captives (to be subsequently
fattened and eaten ; or, if females, for the pleasanter
purpose of matrimony) no doubt existed thousands of
years ago in the wild parts of Negro Africa, and remained sporadic down to the beginning of the present
century. But great " Ghazzias," great warlike expeditions for the collection of hundreds and thousands of
slaves, did not begin—so far as we know—till Islam
was " going strong " in Tropical Africa, in the lands of
the Negroes. The Portuguese and Spaniards were in-
ducted into this business by the Moors ; and the other
maritime peoples of Europe who were colonising
America out-did the Portuguese. And so the New
World came in course of time to have a Negro and
Negroid population of twenty-five millions ; and
interior Africa for at least three centuries was in a state
of continual uproar and devastating tribal conflicts.

Up till the 'thirties and 'forties of the last century
the trade of Africa with the outer world was very
poor : it seemed as though she had little to export save
man-power. But the truly good men—Englishmen,

Scotsmen, French Huguenots, Swedes, Moravians, Anglo-Americans, Danes—who had set themselves to suppress the slave trade, had their practical side. They went out at the close of the eighteenth century—or they sent out men like Mungo Park—to see what else Africa could trade in besides men and women. Their efforts at the time were of course jeered at, just as short-sighted idiots of the present day jeer at the activities of the Anti-Slavery and Aborigines Protection Society. But they had their result a hundred or a hundred and thirty years afterwards, in our own day, in the gigantically increased commerce of Africa with the outer world. Prior to 1819, the money value of yearly African exports to the outer world—setting aside that of the thousands of slaves exported to America, Turkey, Persia and India—scarcely exceeded a total of £1,500,000 per annum. The produce exported consisted of a little gold-dust from the Gold Coast and Senegal; a little ivory from South and West Africa; gum-arabic from Senegal; camwood for dyeing purposes from West Africa; leopard-skins and ostrich plumes and Moorish leather. Nowadays, that is to say in the twelve months which preceded the outbreak of war in 1914, the exports of Africa had risen to a total in annual value of about £164,000,000; and consisted of the following classes of goods:

Vegetable products, chiefly food-stuffs: Maize, durra, millet, barley, wheat, halfa grass, olive oil, ground-nuts (for making other palatable oils and fats), coco-nuts or dried copra, coffee, tea, cocoa, sugar, tobacco, drugs of several kinds, gums, fruits (such as bananas, pine-apples, dates, oranges and lemons, grapes, figs, plums, cherries and almonds), potatoes, wine, oil-seeds, palm oil and palm-kernel oil, shea butter, indigo, dye - woods, cabinet - making woods, cotton of the best quality, rubber, fibre and essences for perfumes.

Mineral products : Gold, tin, copper, magnetic and hæmatite iron, lead, zinc, corundum (aluminium), monazite, coal, phosphates, guano, emery powder and diamonds.

Animal products : Cattle, horses, sheep, goats, mules, asses, camels, hides, wool, mohair, ivory, ostrich feathers, leopard and monkey skins, poultry, quails, beeswax and menagerie animals.

Another great asset of Africa is meteorological : its climate. Although a large part of tropical Equatorial Africa is unhealthy for Europeans, it is only so because of the germ diseases which are present—dormant, so to speak—in the blood of native humans and animals ; but which can be conveyed with intensified virulence to the veins of foreigners not native to Africa, and to the domestic animals they have introduced recently or anciently. The conveying agencies of these diseases are insects and ticks. But when thoroughgoing measures are taken to destroy or avoid these insect pests, no transmission of disease takes place ; in fact, it is well within the purview of science that these germ diseases of the Tropics may be eliminated or nullified by prophylactics. But for the most part they only close a certain proportion of Africa to White colonisation or temporary sojourn for pleasure or profit. The " unhealthy " regions are capable of supporting a large Negro population, and their soil could grow enor-

G

mously valuable food crops. In reference, however, to other areas of Africa it might be said that they possess a positive money-value in their climate. This is especially the case in the northern regions bordering on the Sahara : Morocco, Algeria, Tunis, Tripoli and Egypt ; whither before the war our invalids were passing in ever-increasing numbers to regain health or to ward off the maladies of old age which in our homeland attack us more virulently during the winter half of the year. Other glorious health-restoring climates are the appanage of the greater part of South Africa—all Cape Colony and the Orange River State, nearly all South-west Africa, much of the Transvaal and Natal ; as well as the highlands of Rhodesia and Nyasaland, East Africa (including that portion recently called German), parts of Abyssinia and small portions of the Cameroons. There are also those island paradises off the north-west coast of Africa : Madeira and the Canaries.

The mighty rivers and countless smaller streams and torrents of Africa will play a great rôle in its future development ; not so much because they may provide (as in the Congo basin) cheap transport routes ; as from the very reason which caused us to curse them in the past as the chief obstacles to the " opening up " of Africa : namely, their impassable rapids and innumerable falls and cascades. All over Africa, excepting in the Saharas and the Kalahari deserts, the force of gravitation made manifest by the falling, hurrying water will be harnessed by Man and supply African industries of all kinds with water-power and electricity. The deserts will be subdued by irrigation. We can see this lovely process at work in Egypt and French North

Africa, in the Union of South Africa. Districts that were featureless, sandy wastes a few years since are now corn-fields, maize-fields, orchards, date-groves, cotton plantations, sweet pastures for cattle.

What part in the development of this New Africa is to be played by the Native? After an interval of some years, the principle of the external slave trade with Africa which haunted the European conception of a " colonial " policy was succeeded by the principle of internal slavery. The Americas were closed or closing against the importation of servile labour from Africa. But the European or Europeanised powers then governing Africa had conceived the idea of cultivating or exploiting Africa itself by negro serfs. In Egypt, Abyssinia, Morocco, Zanzibar, the outspoken ruling classes called a slave a slave and treated him not at all badly. In all Moslem Africa, once the initial harm was done of the slave-raid or the provoked inter-tribal war which produced the supply of slaves, once the weary journey to the north or the east was accomplished, the lot of the exiled Negro was an easy and often a happy and honourable one. But in the European-governed Africa of the 'sixties, and even down to the beginning of the twentieth century, the principle of helotry for the indigenous populations under control came into being, though it was disguised under many pleasant names and high-sounding policies. The Negro was to have no rights, no territorial claims in the land of his birth and industry; and the gains or profits resulting from the control of his country were to be spent not on *his* land but on the European state that had taken possession. The " native " was to be the serf of the glebe in exchange for being allowed to live free from the terrors of native rule.

There were exceptions to this treatment, of course. In Cape Colony a franchise was given to Negroes and Negroids, and all over Africa missionaries were at work arguing with their fellow-Europeans for justice to the African. But the general idea among the European powers of those times—1830 to 1910—was to found "colonies" in Africa without much regard for the rights of the native races. The French conquest of Algeria was followed by the pretence that Algeria was henceforth part of France—three more Departments— to be colonised by Frenchmen and Alsatians at all costs. Italy's ambition to acquire Tripoli was based on the belief that she could substitute for one million Libyans and Tibus three million Italian settlers. Spain desired to conquer Morocco in order to populate it with Spaniards. The British wrenched Natal from the Boers not to restore it to the Zulu-Kafir race but to make it a British colony. America spent much money and some valuable lives in buying or conquering Liberia from its stalwart indigenous Negro peoples in order to substitute Aframericans—American-born Negroes and Negroids—for native Vais, Krus, Kpwesis and Grebos.

This unwise and unfair principle in the Development of Africa received its most exaggerated expression at the hands of King Leopold II. (prompted, however, by American, British and German advisers). Under the Congo régime a European power or a mere group of foreign concessionaires arrogated to itself the fee-simple, the sole possession of an African country. The indigenous peoples were denied rights to anything more than the area of the land which they had under cultivation or on which their villages stood. They were to have no voice whatever in the affairs of their country and its government, and were to be compelled to work for little pay or no pay at all in the interests of the foreigner ; while the revenues they assisted to raise were to be spent on distant lands at the caprice of their foreign, self-imposed ruler.

This system, which proved immediately profitable to the foreigner, was rapidly copied in parts of French, British, German and Portuguese Africa, with resultant native risings and punitive expeditions. Fortunately for Africa several influential men arose in this country—Mr. Fox-Bourne, Mr. E. D. Morel, the late Lord Cromer— in France, in the United States, in Italy, in Switzerland and in Belgium, who protested against this wrong system of exploiting Africa, not only because of its inherent conflict with Christian principles, but more cogently still because of its rank unprofitableness. Belgium was awakened to her responsibilities. Many brave Belgians had given their lives to crush the Arab slave trade in the very region where Livingstone had so strongly and so truly denounced its horrors. Their fellow-country-men determined that one form of slavery should not be succeeded by another, and made a clean sweep of the Leopoldian régime. With what result ? That to-day in her great distress thousands and thousands of brave Congolese soldiers have come to the rescue of Belgium in Africa. Not only were the German invaders of Congoland speedily driven out of it, but a large force of Congolese soldiers under Belgian officers has played a most notable part in driving the Germans out of the western half of German East Africa, and has released from an unusually cruel form of imprisonment the captured British missionaries and civilians.

The success of the Morel propaganda led to the reform of conditions in British, French, and Portuguese Africa which might have incurred and did incur the same strictures as were applied to the rule of King Leopold II. We now realise that it doesn't pay to maltreat the African peoples ; that we are there as educators ; as rulers, if you wish ; as investigators ; as traders in very profitable commerce ; as folk who have every right to turn their talents, their superior education and experience to good profit : but not for the purpose of treating the indigenous peoples of Africa —any more than of America or Asia—as of unequal humanity with ourselves. A very happy example of the right and the wrong methods of dealing with Africa may be seen in the progress of Egypt, Tunis and Morocco, under a right system of European guidance, and the former stagnation of Algeria, Turkish Tripoli, Portuguese East Africa under a wrong system. What might be called a clinching argument is the difference between cocoa growing in the Cameroons under more or less servile conditions, and on the Gold Coast by free natives, owners of the ground on which the cacao bushes were planted. In 1912 the German Cameroons' plantations exported *three thousand five hundred* tons of cacao beans, and in the same period of twelve months those belonging to natives of the British Gold Coast exported *thirty-eight thousand* tons.

There is room for a great deal of actual European

colonisation in Africa without injustice or injury to the natives. It is a great mistake to regard Africa as entirely a Black Man's continent, or Asia, America and Australia as destined to be only White or Yellow. There may even arise after this war industrial or commercial colonies of Negroes in Europe specially connected with African interests and industries. Mighty White nations—there is room for them—may grow up in North Africa and in South Africa. One of the wisest remarks I have heard lately as to the importance of Africa was made by the editor of the *Tropical World*. He pointed out that the greatest need of the world after this war would be food-stuffs—a need that will now never slacken as the world's population increases. No continent is so well adapted by soil and climate—properly controlled—for the raising of an infinite variety of food-stuffs as is Africa. Even the Sahara produces the best dates and the best barley. The unhealthy rankness of Equatorial Africa is so much wasted force and energy, which should be purged by the production of nitrogenous vegetation.

But great results can only be achieved by combining in an honest partnership the Black Man's physical strength and immunity from a Tropical sun, the Yellow Man's patient industry and deft fingers, with the White Man's science, grit, and resolve to subdue Nature to his needs. Left to themselves without the interposition and counsels of the White, Black and Yellow would relapse into their internecine struggles for power and property and their devastating wars of religion or blood-lust. Remember also the warnings that German publicists have uttered. They say, after this war, if they can exact a German peace, they will organise all Negro

Africa against the rest of the world and make themselves masters of its huge resources as an instrument in world-domination. This threat alone should lead the Western nations of Europe, the far-sighted Americans and Asiatics, into an alliance with the peoples of Africa to stave off the German menace, and so to develop the incalculable wealth of Africa for the benefit of Africa as well as of Europe, Asia and America.

But if we, above all nations, are to play a great part in Africa as well as in Asia and America, we must educate ourselves, we must specialise—men and women alike—in the subjects needed by a governing and directing race which in its turn is to educate backward peoples and utilise all the resources of this planet in the service of Man. Education at the present moment, after the sheer need to conquer Germany, is our gravest outlook. We who have examined the matter from an imperial stand-point, are not greatly moved by the incessant postpone-ment of new Education Bills, because we realise that they do not go to the root of the matter. They may provide for a much increased amount of time to be given up to youthful education of the masses, but they do not touch the education of the governing classes, and, *worst of all, do not deal with the quality of our education for classes and masses alike.*

It is in the curricula of our schools that we are most at fault. The real enemies of the British people, the real Little-Englanders, the real pro-Germans are the more elderly schoolmasters and pedants, the Masters of Colleges and their pupils the maleducated politicians, journalists and permanent officials who would tie us up still in the swaddling-clothes of the fifteenth century.

" Oh, *why* did they not teach us Modern History and Geography at Winchester ? " wrote to me the other day an officer in high command on the French front. He has taught himself geography, slowly and painfully, in Indian, African and European campaigns, but is only too well aware of his inadequate knowledge of the things that really count in modern warfare and in that political administration which so often goes with warfare in Asia and Africa. I believe originally he got into Sandhurst mainly through his knowledge of the Greek Testament, geography at that time, as now, being so poorly marked in the examinations approved by the War Office that it was hardly worth taking up (it is 600 marks as against 4000 for Greek and Latin). Indeed, the spite shown against geography in education on the part of the Board of Education, the Treasury, the Civil Service Commissioners and all the high authorities that control our education is inexplicable, and is frequently the subject of protest not only on the part of the Royal Geographical Society, but of late actually of the professors of Oxford University. I have recently been at Oxford to renew my own knowledge of certain subjects and to confer with the University Press as to a book of mine on African languages which they are printing. I found, it is true, that all the post offices, head and subordinate, were still engraved with the initials V.R., but although Oxford may not be aware that Queen Victoria is dead, it is becoming alive and alarmed at the growing discrepancy between the requirements of imperial knowledge and the standards of national and class education. There is not much that wants setting right with our Universities ; the faults lie with the quality of our primary and secondary school education. In none of our schools is ethnology taught, the most important of all sciences for an Imperialist—and a boiler-maker and grocer are just as important members of the Empire as a member of Parliament or an editor ; in very few of them is great attention given to the teaching of Botany and the right kind of Botany, the Botany that borders on horticulture, agriculture, forestry and the exploitation of the riches of tropical lands. Before the war nearly all the Botany—the practical Botany of commerce—of the British Empire was done by studious Germans, and admirably well done. They will never do it again. Who is going to take their place ? What encouragements are given by our ill-educated Governments, our old-fashioned Board of Education, our Eton and Balliol Ministers of Education to worthy young men and women to make a great career out of Botany, Ethnology, Linguistics, all branches of Natural Science ? Even the gigantic importance of Chemistry is only dimly appreciated.

Some years ago I was in Guernsey, and in that pleasant land of half-pay retirement I met a maiden lady at a garden party with a name that caught my ear and at once suggested visions of an amazing flora on the Cameroons and the Himalayas. " Is it possible," I said, in almost trembling accents, " that you can be a relation of the great Dr. ——, who was Government Botanist in West Africa and India ? " " Oh *dear* no ! " she said, much offended, " WE were always MILITARY people."

We want soldiers and sailors just as much as we want

botanists and chemists. It is no good working up the cultivation of our homeland or our colonies if we cannot defend them. But what we have got to fight against is this silly depreciation of Modern Science, this stale superstition that the career of arms is more showy, more honourable than enrolment in the army which fights a tougher enemy than Man : grudging, recalcitrant, remorseless Nature, that slowly receding Force which stands between the human race and the Millennium, the Dragon that guards the Treasure of the Gods.

CHAPTER VI

PROBLEMS OF THE PACIFIC

By BASIL THOMSON, C.B.

THE Pacific Ocean—the widest ocean on the globe—falls naturally into two parts ; the northern portion is almost destitute of islands : a ship sailing along the latitude of 30° North, from China to the western shore of North America, will navigate for nearly 7000 miles without sighting land ; the southern portion is dotted with islands, more and more thickly as one travels westward. The islands in the Pacific, in fact, are geographically more nearly connected with Australia and New Zealand than with any part of the great continents that enclose the ocean. With some insignificant exceptions all these islands lie within the tropics. Climate is apt to have the last word in determining the fate of nations. It is a disturbing reflection that if the temperature of the globe were to rise or to fall a paltry forty degrees Fahrenheit there would be an end of civilisation, if not of the human race, and a lesser change of climate within historical times has ended in disaster over limited areas such as the Khotan desert in Central Asia, which supported a thriving and cultured population in the first century A.D. and is now an uninhabitable waste of shifting sand. The climate of most of the islands is dependent upon the south-east trade wind. This wind used to blow with fair regularity over the whole area from March to October. But the older inhabitants assert that during the last fifty years it has decreased both in force and regularity, and even during the fine winter months there are days when the wind sets in from the west and north-west with heavy rain. During the summer months weeks may pass with low-lying rain-clouds and moist heat. It is a flat calm, with the thermometer at ninety, and life becomes a burden even to the natives. After the calm there is a westerly gale, and sometimes, especially in December and March, the islands are swept bare by cyclones. The trade wind is sensitive to the influence of land : even small islands only a few feet above sea level, like the Paumotus, have a marked effect upon its regularity. In the larger islands, owing to the cooling of the surface in the night, the trade wind dies down after sunset, and a land breeze sets in, allowing small craft, which have been lying snugly at anchor all day, to creep eastward along the coast until daybreak, although a few miles out the adverse trade wind may be blowing as fiercely as ever.

The south-east trade wind blows in a broad belt from the equator nearly to New Zealand. North of the line the trade wind is north-east as far as a few degrees north of Hawaii. North of this line the wind blows from the south-west. About New Guinea, and as far as the northern Solomon Islands the north-west monsoon prevails in the summer months. These facts, all-important as they were in the time of the Spaniards, ceased to have importance with the coming of the steamship, but they will come into great prominence again in aerial travel of the future.

The approach of a cyclone is announced by the barometer. The mercury begins to fall rapidly, and even to rise and fall visibly like the action of a pump. The birds show by their behaviour that they feel the approach of danger. The wind rises to a gale ; the rain descends like a water-spout. When the cyclone is at its height the velocity of the wind may attain eighty-five miles an hour. After blowing thus for four or five hours the blast suddenly ceases, and the air is so still that a match may be lighted out of doors. Throughout the fifteen minutes of this deceptive calm there is a continuous roar in the upper air. Then there is a sharp puff of wind from the opposite quarter, and the natives know that the centre of the storm has passed over them, and that the worst is yet to come. In a few minutes the storm is upon them from the opposite quarter—this time with redoubled fury. Native huts that have been forced into a slanting position towards the west are now blown to a corresponding angle the other way. The path of these circular storms is not very wide. Observations taken in Fiji show that the hurricane itself is seldom more than sixty miles wide, though a strong gale may extend to twice that width. While the velocity of the wind is eighty or ninety miles an hour, the rate of progression of the gigantic eddy is only ten miles an hour. This knowledge enables navigators to steer out of its path, but the hapless islanders crawl out of their shelters to find their coco-nut trees stripped, their bananas uprooted, their houses unroofed and demolished, their cane-fields laid flat, and their food-plantations washed away by floods or by tidal waves. Happily the climate and the soil are in their favour, and the islands recover from cyclones far sooner than would be possible in any other country.

The rainfall in the islands is high, but a high annual rainfall does not connote an excessive number of wet days. The rainfall varies from 130 inches in the Solomon Islands to 81 in the Cook group, but more than 8 inches may fall in a single day, as in Fiji in October, 1910. During the winter months, from June to August, weeks may pass without a drop of rain. At such times the plants get their moisture from the heavy dew.

The South Sea Islands cover an area about 4000 miles from east to west and 3000 miles from north to south. Their physical conformation is infinitely varied. Many of the smaller islands are built of coral, either as atolls, like Ducie Island, elevated but a few feet above high-water mark and enclosing a lagoon, or like the neighbouring island, Henderson, as elevated plateaux of dead coral, upheaved eighty feet above the sea. In some cases volcanic rock is extruded through the coral so as to form a mountainous core, fringed by limestone cliffs, as in Vavau ; in others the reef has been raised scarce twenty feet, as in Tongatabu ; in others again the whole island is formed of volcanic material, with or without a fringing reef of coral. In fact, the formation of all these archipelagoes may be traced directly or indirectly to volcanic agency, perhaps at a not very remote geological period. In the island of Tanna, in the New Hebrides, in the Tongan group, and in Niuafo'ou there are active volcanoes ; hot springs are found in Fiji and in other islands. Changes of level have taken place in historical times. During an eruption in Tonga in 1886 Falcon Reef, over which the sea normally broke at high water, discharged a mass of pumice which formed an island from eighty to one hundred feet high. The Tongan flag was planted on it almost before it was cool, but the King of Tonga drew no revenue from it, for it was entirely washed away by the waves in 1898. In Vatulele (Fiji), an upheaved reef island, one may see, cut deep into the cliff face some twenty feet above high-water mark, a continuous gallery, eroded by the waves before the island was suddenly thrust up to its present level. In the caves that honeycomb these coral islands the stalagmitic columns are sometimes cut asunder as if a slice had been taken out of them with a sharp knife, either near the roof, or midway, or near the floor. The edges are free from any deposit of stalactite, which shows that the change in level must have been quite recent. Detached coral barriers like the Astrolabe and Indispensable Reefs, stretching like nets across the path of shipping, have destroyed many vessels ; for at night there is nothing to warn the approaching ship of her danger except the sound of the breakers, inaudible in heavy weather, or, when the wind is in the right direction, the smell of the reef itself. In coral seas, however, there is a compensation for the dangers of sunken reefs in the multitude of safe harbours to which the reef forms a natural breakwater. It is the peculiarity of coral that it cannot build in a sea diluted with fresh water ; consequently there is a break in the reef opposite to the mouth of every stream, and through these openings vessels can pass to a safe anchorage, and find fresh water to replenish their casks close to their moorings.

The scenery of the islands, as might be expected from the nature of the material, is of extraordinary beauty and variety. When the volcanic islands are of any size they are heavily timbered on the windward side, almost to the highest peak, and the rainfall is sufficient to feed cascades and streams of limpid water even in the driest season. On the lee side the slopes are clothed with grass, and dotted with clumps of timber like an English park. The course of the mountain stream, here dashing in cascades from rock to rock, and filling deep pools so clear that every rounded pebble on the bottom may be counted ; there foaming through a deep ravine, arched with branches and dappled with shafts of sunshine, is a fairyland. Great vines trail from the leafy vault, or twine about the smooth columns of the *dakua* trees ; tree-ferns rear their coronets in every glade ; feathery bamboos sway rustling in the breeze. At a break in the foliage there is a glimpse of the ocean and the undulating line of the barrier reef white with foam. In the upheaved coral islands the scenery changes. Here there is no running water : the copious rainfall is swallowed by the porous rock to collect in natural cisterns underground, but the scenery is no less enchanting in another fashion. The dense vegetation is intersected with broad grass-roads or narrow paths, which lead one quite suddenly into a coco-nut grove. Beyond is a clearing, shaded by palms and bread-fruit trees, and a neat row of thatched huts or whitewashed cottages. Through the palm-trees one may see the white beach, with the canoes drawn up in a row above high-water mark.

Nature is not always in sunny mood. There are days when the rain descends in cataracts, and the mountain masses are veiled in cloud and sodden with water.

H

Then the tinkling stream is transformed into a roaring torrent ; water-worn boulders are torn from their beds and washed down the channel ; the larger rivers overflow all the low-lying land in their deltas, and deposit silt over the roots of the mangroves, converting the swamps into dry and very fertile land. Most of the native tribes preserve oral traditions of such a flood, and this has formed the text for the argument of some of the early missionaries that the natives had preserved a memory of the Deluge which only Noah and his sons survived.

No picture of island scenery in the Pacific can omit the reef. One is not allowed to forget it. In every glimpse of the sea it lies in the middle distance as an irregular line of white foam following the trend of the coast-line about a mile out to sea. Night and day the roar of the " league-long roller " is heard in a muttered undertone, and when the undertone rises to a booming roar the natives foretell bad weather. In some of the islands an unusual roar of the reef is a death-portent for the ruling family. When a heavy sea is breaking, the line of the reef may be traced by the bank of spray that shrouds the breakers in a shimmering mist. When the wind is blowing from the shore the rollers take on a new beauty : their white crests stream backward like horses' manes as they fling themselves impotently on the sullen barrier of coral. Above high-water mark there is a belt of dazzling white sand, composed of minute particles of shell, and beyond, without any intervening region of dune or grass, the forest begins suddenly. Wherever the shore slopes down to the water's edge there is always a luxuriant growth of trees, whose roots must be drawing their sustenance from the salt water.

I have been a little tedious in dwelling on the climate and scenery, because I believe that they will have a marked influence on the future destiny of the islands. They explain the extraordinary fascination that they have for Europeans, particularly the European city-dweller. No one can describe the life of the settler as luxurious; on the contrary it is full of hardship; but the humbler settler is well content to end his life there, and when he is impelled by force of circumstances to go back to civilised lands, he is very apt to drift back to the islands. Man is naturally a lazy animal, and when he finds himself living in a country where doing nothing in particular has been reduced by the natives to a fine art, he submits to the influence of climate and example without any protest. If the islands could be unmoored and towed, climate and all, to a day's steam from Europe, all other holiday resorts would be deserted. They have already begun to show signs of becoming the holiday resort for Australia and New Zealand, and if improvements in the navigation of air and sea bring them nearer, their population of Europeans, both fleeting and permanent, will greatly increase.

It is essential that in considering the problems of the Pacific we shall take long views. Looking far into the future is an irresponsible proceeding, for who can read the forecasts of former generations without smiling? We are all apt to overestimate the significance of the passing phases of social and economic affairs around us. In England there was revolution in the air in 1793, in 1830 and in 1848, and we have read and smiled at the prophecies of the men of those days. To-day there is the ferment of revolution—true, it is in the columns of a leading newspaper—and the prophet is at work again. He was at work in the islands when I was living there. The Pacific Islands were to make everybody's fortune out of tropical produce. Labour was cheap. The difficulty was not in making things grow, but in stopping them from growing. But experience has shown that even these favoured islands are not exempt from the curse of Adam. To make a fortune, to make even a decent living, a man had to work and to work hard. It is true that almost every kind of tropical produce will thrive in the islands. The cultivation of sugar by Indian coolie labour has been highly developed in Fiji. Copra (the sun-dried kernel of the coco-nut, from which the oil for candles and soap is derived) is a staple industry of the natives in nearly all the islands ; coffee flourished before it was attacked by the disease ; tea grows well on the highlands of Fiji ; tobacco, cinchona, maize, cotton, rubber, rice and ramie fibre have all been successfully grown, and certain local products such as the sea-slug—bêche de mer—which is a delicacy among the Chinese, tortoise-shell, mother-of-pearl, sandal-wood, the trochus shell, used in the manufacture of buttons, have all been exported in a limited quantity. The valuable discovery of rock phosphates is quite recent. This chemical manure lies in beds from one to four feet thick over a number of remote islands which were otherwise commercially valueless. The geological history of these beds is not perfectly established, but they are generally supposed to have been formed by the filtration of a solution of rain-water and guano deposited by sea-birds into the loose-grained coral of which the islands are composed. Wherever native labour can be obtained the rock phosphate is very easy to quarry and ship, especially where there is a natural anchorage. The discovery has led to the annexation of a number of scattered islands that would otherwise not have been worth claiming. Ocean, Starbuck, Wreck Reef, Cato, Suwarrow, Bird, Jarvis, Enderbury and McKean Islands have been leased to the Pacific Islands Company for terms sufficiently long to allow the deposits to be removed. When they are completely denuded they will doubtless sink back into their old remote isolation. The difficulty in inducing native labour to leave their islands for such uncongenial labour had been increasing before the war, and with the present deficiency of tonnage it must be many years before the profitable export of rock phosphates can be resumed. Except in the French island of New Caledonia there is no mining in the Pacific Islands, though it is quite likely that when the Solomon Islands come to be fully explored, ores will be discovered. Manufactures have been neglected hitherto. Even in Fiji, which has been a British colony for nearly fifty years, and timber, clay and building stone are plentiful, nearly all the buildings have been constructed of imported materials. It is remarkable that in that colony copra, the raw material for soap-making, is exported to Europe, and soap, to the annual value of £1600, is brought all the way from England, when a small factory on the spot would have the advantages of cheap material, cheap labour, a local market and no charges for freight. The reason is that the local island market is too small to justify capitalists in training workmen and in laying down the plant necessary for equipping a factory.

Since the world needs tropical products which thrive luxuriantly in the islands, it is natural to ask why they are not abounding in material prosperity. The answer may be given in the single word—labour. The natives are agriculturists, each cultivating his own land, held either individually or in common. As long as their land produces all that they require, why should they work for foreigners at uncongenial labour ? Very early in the history of European settlement the planters found it necessary to import labour from the islands that had not yet attracted Europeans. Throughout the seventies and eighties of the last century Melanesian and Micronesian labourers were recruited for the plantations of Fiji and New Caledonia on a contract of service for a term of years and repatriation at the end of the term with wages in the form of " trade " goods. In its early stages this traffic was full of abuses. There were charges of kidnapping and outrage, and if these charges were sometimes exaggerated by philanthropic critics, there can be no doubt that many of the labourers did not understand the contract ; that they were often forced on board the labour schooner by their own people, and that they were sometimes landed at a part of the coast belonging to their hereditary foes. Even when the traffic was regulated by the government, and a government agent was carried by each schooner, and the plantations subjected to rigid inspection, the mortality of the labourers from diseases new to them or from nostalgia was very high. About 1880 arrangements were made with the Indian Government to recruit Indian coolies for Fiji. The contract was for five years' service on the plantation at one shilling a day, and five years' residence in the islands before the coolie was entitled to a free passage back to India, and these terms were so attractive that the Indians now number 40,000. Many of the coolies have settled permanently in the islands as sugar-growers on their own account, as pedlars and small shopkeepers. They bring their own women, and so far they have shown but little inclination to intermarriage with the natives, but they form a distinct community. In 1916, however, the Indian Government decided not to allow any further recruiting of indentured labourers, and the labour question has again become a very serious problem.

It is difficult to see how the problem can ever be solved in our generation. The climate is too hot for field labour by Europeans. The islands are too remote from markets to compete with produce grown by cheap labour in tropical countries nearer to Europe, and it appears now that the production of sugar, which absorbs so much capital and labour, will be very much reduced. The export of copra and bananas and many of the minor products will continue since they require no large central factory, and natives have themselves shown a disposition to make money by cultivating their land for the purpose of export.

The scenery does not fully account for the attraction of the islands for Europeans. To explain the sensation produced in Europe in the latter half of the eighteenth century when the accounts of Tahiti by Wallis and Cook were published we must turn to the natives. They belong to three distinct races—the

Malayo-Polynesians, who inhabit all the islands east of Fiji, and speak a common root language with dialectic variations ; the Melanesians, who inhabit the islands west of Fiji, and the Micronesians, a mixed race of uncertain origin, who are found on the small Equatorial islands. Fiji is the meeting-ground of the Polynesians and Melanesians.

The average Polynesian is tall, slim and handsome, light brown in colour and with wavy hair. He is not prognathous, and his features are often of the European cast. He attaches great importance to purity of blood, and he has been so long accustomed to an aristocratic form of government that he has acquired a polished ease of manner that is wanting in the ruder Melanesians. He is friendly and welcoming to Europeans, whom he treats as equals, though he is quick to detect any lack of breeding in his visitors. Most of the Polynesians have adopted European clothing, in which they appear to worse advantage than when they wore the dignified dress of bark cloth, and they are inclined to adopt wooden and concrete bungalows instead of their thatched houses. In general they are inclined to pay to Europeans the flattery of imitation.

The Melanesians, on the other hand, are conservative. They have never taken very kindly to the settlement of Europeans on their islands, nor have they shown much disposition to adopt European customs. Even the labourers who wore European dress while they were working on plantations or on ships, distribute their finery and go back to native undress as soon as they return to their homes. They vary a good deal in colour. In Vanikoro, for instance, they are nearly black ; in the

Solomons there is every gradation of colour from black to red-brown, even in the same island. The hair is frizzy like that of the Fijian, but the pure Melanesian is shorter and stouter in build, and more energetic and industrious. Though there are headmen in all the Melanesian islands, they wield less authority than the chiefs of Polynesia and Fiji, and the Melanesian instinct is republican rather than aristocratic.

The Fijian, who may be said to be a hybrid between the two races, is a man of fine physique, muscular and athletic, with a dark brown skin and frizzy hair, which he dyes with lime, and dresses out until it forms an enormous golden aureole round his head. He is singularly conservative in small matters. His loin-cloth, which for convenience is now made of calico, has never been discarded in favour of trousers ; he still lives in the thatched hut which contented his fathers, and prefers the digging-stick to the spade for cultivating his plantation.

The Micronesian seems to have some Malayan affinities, but there has been so much Polynesian inter-marriage that one may trace in the same village two or more racial types. The Gilbert Islander is short and stoutly built, rather long in the body in proportion to the legs, with eyes set at an oblique angle, a brown skin, and straight black hair which is worn long. He is the most expert and daring fisherman in the Pacific. Unlike the other South Sea races he is prone to sudden gusts of anger, to excessive jealousy and to murderous affrays. Until about 1900 the Gilbert Islanders suffered from chronic over-population of their barren and waterless islands, but latterly there has been a heavy fall in the birth-rate.

This is not the place to touch upon the many points of sociological interest that are to be found among these races, except in so far as they affect the problems of the future. The complicated laws of marriage and relationship, of land tenure and succession to property, of religion and superstition, are a very valuable index to the history of human institutions, but they have no more direct bearing upon the destiny of the islands than the British Museum upon the political history of Great Britain. What does matter is the vitality of the natives, and the part they will be able to play in the social development of the next few generations. It is probable that the native population of all the islands is either stationary or decreasing. It is the fashion to assert that native races begin to decline as soon as they come into contact with Europeans. This arises from our evil modern habit of making false generalisations. The fact that some isolated races decrease rapidly soon after Europeans settle among them is so dramatic that we eagerly fasten on the generalisation that the weaker races are doomed to extinction before the all-conquering European, forgetting the steady increase of the Bantu races in Africa, of the Indians and the Chinese up to and even beyond the limit of population which their country can support. The main cause for the sudden decrease of a race is the introduction of new diseases, which assume a more virulent aspect when they strike root in a virgin soil. This affects an insular far more than a continental race. But we are now beginning to learn that this condition is only temporary. For a generation or so a race seems to sicken and pine like an individual, but like an individual it may recover. The turning-point may come when the race has been reduced by four-fifths, like the Maories, or to a mere handful like the blacks of New South Wales, but there comes a time when the decay is arrested. True, fusion with another race may set in, and the pure type be lost ; but the blood remains.

The population of the South Sea Islands has, if we may judge from Fiji, where births and deaths have been registered for more than forty years, decreased by half during the last half-century, and probably now it is less than one million. The birth-rate is still fairly high, and the mortality is principally among infants who die of whooping-cough and other European diseases. There are now signs that the decrease has stopped. This handful of natives—for it is only a handful relatively to the extent of the islands—owns practically all the land. Whenever it is necessary in Fiji to acquire land for public purposes the land is leased, and the tribal owners divide the rent among them. It is not, therefore, at all likely that any large body of coloured settlers will be attracted to the islands in order to culti-vate vacant lands, for though much of the land is un-cultivated, none of it can be said to be vacant. The Pacific Islander is always earth-hungry, and one has only to look at a plot of his uncultivated land for him to discover that it is the one spot suited to his next year's plantation.

To describe the native as conservative does not mean that he is incapable of progress. He is in bondage to the law of custom, as all primitive races have been until they were shaken out of the groove by a stimulus from without. If you read Catoira's account of Mendaña's ex-ploration of the Solomon Islands in 1568, and compare it with what we now know of the natives in our own time, you will see that in every particular, down to the pettiest detail in their dress, their daily life and their language, they had not stirred a finger for three hundred years. Now, they are making up for the lost time. In those three centuries we know that there must have been rare souls, born before their time, in whom the eternal " Thou shalt not " of the law of custom provoked the question " Why ? " They met the fate ordained for all such men, which in civilised states is the hemlock, the cross and the stake ; in uncivilised the club and the spear. Perhaps the real complaint against Socrates was that a continuous flow of reproof is more than erring man can endure, but the published grounds for his condemnation were that he denied the gods recognised by the state and that he corrupted the young. Reformers never lived long among primitive races : if they were low-born they were clubbed, and that was the end of them and their reforms ; if they were chiefs, and something happened to them either by accident or disease, men saw therein the finger of an offended deity, and obedience to the existing order of things became stronger than before. This was specially so among ancestor-worshippers like the Melanesians, for dead ancestors, seeing their customs derided, were sure to show their displeasure by bringing pestilence or bad harvests.

The question of what part is to be played by natives in the future development of the Pacific is not confined to the Pacific Islands. It concerns the peoples of all the lands bordering on the great ocean—the Japanese, Chinese and Malays as well as the people of Aryan descent in America and Australia and New Zealand.

The present population of the globe is believed to be about fifteen hundred millions, of which seven hundred millions are nominally progressive and eight hundred millions are stagnant under the law of custom. Are these eight hundred millions, who happen for the moment to be politically inferior to the other seven hundred millions, for ever to remain hewers of wood and drawers of water ? Are they unprogressive owing to inherent incapacity ? If this question had been asked seventy or eighty years ago we know what the answer would have been. The Japanese as well as the Chinese would have been classed among the unprogressive races, but we all know of the marvellous internal regeneration that in a period of less than forty years has raised Japan to the importance of a first-class power. I am beginning to doubt whether any uncivilised race is really inferior in capacity to Europeans. I think it was Professor Flinders Petrie who expressed the view that the average man cannot absorb more knowledge than his immediate ancestors, and that the growth of the mind can in the average man be but by fractional increments in each generation. He gave as an instance the Egyptian peasant who has been taught to read and write, and described him as " silly, half-witted and incapable of taking care of himself," while the Copt, whose ancestors have been scribes for generations, can be educated without ill effect. I venture to think that there are more exceptions than will prove any such rule. I believe that Maori children, when they can be induced to work, are not inferior in ability to their white school-fellows : certainly the Tongans, another branch of the Poly-nesian race, learn in their own island to write shorthand

and solve problems in higher mathematics. Fijian boys educated in Sydney have proved to be equal to the average : New Guinea children do very well in the mission schools : Booker Washington and Dubois are two out of a number of negroes of high attainments. And if we turned to the more backward races, Australian aborigines and even Andaman Islanders are said to have shown aptitude when they have overcome the difficulty of a common language with their teacher. The Masai are the most backward of the East African tribes, yet I remember reading that the Government Secretary of Uganda employed two Masai boys to develop his photographs. In all uncivilised races one finds a lack of application, and few of them will submit to the confinement necessary for serious study. I believe that all races are teachable, but it is character rather than intellect that achieves things in this world, and it takes many generations of habit and example to build up character. In one of his letters to Atticus Cicero warns his friend against admitting British slaves to his household on account of their crass stupidity.

While all races are teachable, there are racial idiosyncrasies which we are only beginning to discover. Why, for instance, should the Hausa and the Sudanese have a natural liking for European military discipline, while the Waganda find it irksome ? Why do the Masai, whose development is Palæolithic in its simplicity, make trustworthy policemen and prison warders, while the Somalis have been found utterly worthless in both capacities ? Why are the Maoris and·Solomon Islanders natural artists in wood-carving, while the tribes most nearly allied to them are almost destitute of artistic skill ?

These natural aptitudes will begin to make themselves felt as soon as these people have shaken off the fetters of custom, and have entered into free competition with the rest of mankind.

Before this can happen we shall have to get rid of race-contempt. It is impossible to believe that a white skin is to be for ever a sort of patent of nobility in the world-state of the future. I do not think that the psychology of race-contempt has ever been dispassionately studied. It is felt most strongly in the United States and the West Indies ; a little less strongly in the other British tropical possessions. In England it is sporadic, and is generally confined to the educated classes. It is scarcely noticeable in France, Spain, Portugal or Italy. From this it might be argued that it is peculiar to races of Teutonic origin, were it not for the fact that Germans in tropical countries do not seem to feel it. It is a sentiment of quite modern growth. In the fifteenth and sixteenth centuries Englishmen did not regard coloured people as their inferiors by reason of the colour of their skin. It appears, in fact, to date only from the time of negro slavery in the West Indies, and yet the Romans, the Spaniards and the Portuguese, who were the greatest slave-owners in history, never held marriage with coloured people in contempt. The only race-hatred in the Middle Ages was against the gypsies and the Jews, and this was due to the Crusader spirit. The colour line is drawn more firmly by men than by women, and deep-seated as it is in the Southern States just now, it may be nothing more than a passing phase of sentiment, a sub-conscious instinct of self-preservation in a race which feels that its old predominance is threatened by equality with its former servants. If you analyse the sentiment it comes to this. You may tolerate the coloured man in every relation but one : you may converse with him, eat with him, live with him on terms of equality, but your gorge rises at the idea of admitting him into your family by marriage. There are a few hints in classical literature of a dislike for mixed marriages, but the antipathy seems to have been against alliances between Roman citizens and barbarians. A Roman citizen who took a British woman to wife would have been condemned equally with him who wedded an Ethiopian. It was certainly not an instinct three centuries ago, for Shakespeare had no fear of alienating the sympathies of his audience by marrying Desdemona to a man of colour. Early in the sixteenth century Sieur Paulmier de Gonneville of Normandy gave his heiress in marriage to Essomeric, the son of a Brazilian chief, and no one thought that she was hardly treated. It is not a pleasant subject to dwell upon, but it is a fact that women of Anglo-Saxon blood do, even in these days, mate with Chinese, Arabs, Kaffirs and even Negroes, despite the active opposition of their relations. History is filled with romantic examples of the marriage of European men with native women, to cite no more than de Bethancourt with the Guanche princess; Cortes with his Mexican interpreter; John Rolfe with Pocahontas. It is the fashion to describe the half-caste offspring of such marriages as having all the vices of both races and none of the virtues. In so far as this accusation is true, it is accounted for by the social ostracism in which half-castes are condemned to live. But it seems now to be established that in intellectual aptitude as well as in physical endowment the half-caste is equal to the average European when he has the same educational opportunities, and that there is no physical deterioration in the offspring of the marriage of half-castes *inter se*.

Race prejudice does not die so hard as one would think. Let the European find himself alone and dependent on the goodwill of coloured people, and you find him at once treating them with deference and respect. It will be so in the Pacific at a not very distant day. There, as in temperate zones, wealth will create a new aristocracy recruited from men of every shade of colour. We shall see men of Hindu and Japanese and Chinese and native origin controlling industries with their wealth as Europeans now control the commerce of India and China, and as the aristocracy will be composed of every shade of colour, so will be the masses of men who work with their hands. In one place the majority of the labourers will be brown or yellow ; in another white ; but white men will work side by side with men of colour and feel no degradation.

It is often said that the Panama Canal will greatly affect the destiny of the Pacific. It will appreciably shorten the voyage from Europe to Australia and the Far East, but I think that it will affect the islands no more than the opening of the Suez Canal affected Diego Garcia. The natives of a few islands will see great liners steaming in the offing and will pursue their occupations as placidly as the ploughman in the Midlands who sees the Scotch express thundering northward through his valley. A few islands, now among the most inaccessible on the globe, may be dragged into

I

the vortex, like Fanning Island, which is now a busy cable station. The aerial traffic of the future will need landing stations for the journey across the Pacific, and some of us may live to see a modern hotel and aerial garage built among the megalithic monuments of Easter Island. But for several generations to come the great majority of the islands will probably play a humble part in the world's progress as tropical kitchen-gardens and holiday-grounds for Australia and New Zealand.

Not long ago the German Colonial Minister—then a minister without portfolio—declared that Germany must have back her colonies in the Pacific. I can well understand his desire, for he was the first governor of German Samoa, and the founder of a new German policy towards the natives in those islands. Seventeen years ago it fell to me to take over from the Germans certain shadowy German interests in Tonga on behalf of our Government, and I was Dr. Solf's guest for a few days in Samoa. He confided to me that he intended in Samoa, as in his earlier administration in German East Africa, to copy the British methods of dealing with the natives, and he asked me to send him all the native laws passed in Fiji and Tonga as a model for his own code. His great difficulty was money, and he told me that with all the expenditure lavished by the German Government on subsidising steamships in the Pacific, he could not hope to get from the Reichstag the funds necessary for colonial administration. Dr. Solf was quite the ablest of German colonial administrators, and I was not surprised to hear that he had gone to the Colonial Office. He was to have visited London in

August, 1914, and I remember von Kühlmann telling me that many people had marked him out for the next Chancellor.

It is, I believe, a common belief that German colonial administration is stained with injustice and cruelty to the natives. Such charges are made against every colonial power in turn. In the early days of colonising the Germans put down native resistance harshly and brutally. It has always been part of their policy to emulate the Huns in such matters, but when things are running smoothly their tendency has been to indulgence and over-familiarity with the natives, and as a consequence they have failed to win their respect as they had already failed to win their affection. Whatever may be the case in other German colonies, I do not think that in the Pacific they can be accused of frightening away German settlers by over-government. Nevertheless they do not attract a German population, and there was no disposition on the part of Germans settled in the neighbouring British colonies to remove to islands governed by their own countrymen. It is a fact much deplored by German writers that Germans living under the British flag very quickly lose their sense of nationality, and adopt the views of the people among whom they live. Under the strain of a war like this it is possible that the sense of German nationality and patriotism may reassert itself in individuals, but, as has recently been discovered in the United States, the great mass of Germans, naturalised and unnaturalised, have thrown in their lot with the country of their adoption. Though the fire of patriotism may burn fiercely in German hearts, as German newspapers are never tired of assuring us, a remarkable number of German deserters are ready and even eager to give their enemies information most damaging to the interests of their government.

There are many reasons why Dr. Solf will have to be disappointed. His disappointment is easy to understand (though the commercial value of the German colonies in the Pacific is not very great), for it was a German firm that first organised the trade of the Pacific Islands.

In the early seventies the great Hamburg firm of Godefroy had agents for produce in almost every group. Their agents had very careful instructions to abstain from mixing in native politics, and to devote themselves solely to getting all the trade into their hands. Their modern representatives still have agencies in Polynesia, but much of their business has got into the hands of English colonial firms, and twenty years ago a German steamer, subsidised by the German Government, solemnly ploughed her way from island to island with empty holds, while the German traders were loading the Sydney and Auckland steamers to the hatchways.

Few of the larger groups of islands now belong to the nation that discovered them. The British flag was hoisted over Tahiti and New Caledonia, which now belong to the French ; over Hawaii, which is American ; and over what was German New Guinea. The Solomon Islands and the New Hebrides were formally annexed by Spain. The periods of discovery fall naturally into centuries. The sixteenth century belongs to the Spanish, the seventeenth to the Dutch and the eighteenth to the French and the English, but neither the Spanish or the Dutch now hold any territory in the Pacific. The

Germans were the last to come, at the period of what the newspapers called the " scramble for Hinterlands " in the last quarter of the nineteenth century, and they took all the unattached groups as part of their policy of acquiring a place in the sun. The British Government, on the other hand, acquired its territory with reluctance. It refused the offer of Fiji in 1860, though it was driven by pressure from the English settlers to accept it fourteen years later. It would have acquiesced under protest in the annexation of New Guinea by Germany had it not been for the pressure exerted by the Australians. It declined the offer of Samoa, and it is only within the last few years that under the persuasion of the New Zealanders it has taken over the Cook Group, Savage Island, and a large number of small islands which are rich in rock phosphates. But England is the only Power in the Pacific which has a large and increasing white population near the islands. The French settlements in Tahiti, the Marquesas and New Caledonia are political colonies in the sense that the will to annex them came from the Home Government, and not from the colonists. The most valuable on account of its mines is New Caledonia, and that was primarily a penal colony. The German colonies were even more artificial, and if the governments of Australia and New Zealand insist, as they have the will and the right to insist, that they shall not be returned to the Germans, the German occupation of them will pass into history as an episode of no importance to any one except the natives, who have welcomed the ejectment of their German masters. For it is not a question of national vanity, but a fact beyond all dispute, that the natives of the Pacific prefer the English to all other Europeans. Some years ago I remember overhearing Tukuaho, a high Tongan chief, mimicking the speech and manners of Germans and Frenchmen. It was a most realistic performance ; the words were gibberish, but the accent was perfect. I expected a personation of the Englishman to follow, and I asked him afterwards why he had omitted it. He seemed surprised, and said, " There is nothing funny about the Englishman. He is our friend." It is to this subtle distinction that the success of British administrators in the Pacific is to be attributed.

If I now venture into the region of prophecy, and try to take long views of the future of the Pacific, I shall not seem more irresponsible than the host of political prophets who have lately come to grief. Prophets—especially war-prophets—have had experiences lately that should teach them caution for the rest of their days, and if we embark upon forecasts and the course of history stultifies us, we shall look foolish in good company. Four great nations are vitally concerned in the Pacific—England, the United States, Japan and China. I leave out France purposely, because her island colonies depend so little upon commercial interests. Of these four we may leave out China. The Chinese are colonists, but politically they are not a colonising nation. The United States have, as it were, acquired their colonies—Hawaii and the Philippines—in the Pacific against their inclination. There remain England and Japan—both maritime nations with the colonising instinct. Japan has already taken temporary charge of the German colonies north of the Equator, and she has the advantage over other nations of being in a position to provide cheap and efficient labour for any tropical possession. For the present her eyes are turned westward towards China, but it is impossible not to feel that if she ever becomes persuaded that colonies in the Pacific are necessary for her growing population, she may become a strong competitor. Changes move so rapidly in Japan that it is quite possible that the quasi-military oligarchy by which she is now controlled may give place to a democracy; there are already whispers of a socialist movement, but the government of the day looks far beyond the shores of Japan for its destiny.

The immediate future of the islands south of the Equator is quite obvious. On the one hand we have all the important groups, with the exception of the French colonies of Tahiti, the Marquesas and New Caledonia, under the British flag: on the other hand we have Australia and New Zealand awakened to their interest in taking over and administering the islands: and, though there has in the past been a disposition to place the administration in the hands of unsuitable persons because they have rendered political services, latterly the choice of administrators has been wise. Fiji is still a Crown Colony, and some of the groups and smaller islands are still under the High Commissioner for the Western Pacific, but it is only a question of time when the natives of Fiji, who might justly claim that under the Deed of Cession they were promised direct administration from England, will desire to come under the same form of colonial government that they see working in the other groups. It is even possible that the next generation may live to see a federation of the islands with a separate legislature under the British flag.

It has been said, and with some justice, that a democracy, and especially a republican democracy, is not fitted to administer a widely scattered empire over coloured races. It may not be the soil best suited to the growth of such an empire, but the belief is one of those philosophic generalities which warp political judgment. Everything depends upon the genius of the people who compose the democracy. It is quite true that the full growth of the Roman Empire was not attained until Rome had passed from a democracy into a military dictatorship, but the foundations of the empire had been laid long before this, and in our own time the French have shown how, under entirely democratic institutions at home, the administration of coloured races may successfully be achieved. Our own institutions are democratic enough, and we see the Empire to-day composed of almost independent democracies, each grappling with the native problem within its frontiers with success, and welded together by sentiment and interest in a way which has been the astonishment of the common enemy and of the world. If there is the instinct of good order, sound and incorrupt administration, honesty and justice in the blood, then I say that a democracy need not fear to take up the burden of empire, nor will its enemies do wisely in counting upon any weakness in the form of government to serve their ends. Whether it is finally decided that the German colonies pass to the League of Nations with a mandate to Australia and New Zealand to administer them, or are incorporated in those colonial states, is a matter of small importance.